Praise

'Whether you are a developing or experienced coach, the MAGIC model provides an excellent framework to help guide your coaching conversations. This brilliant book is pragmatic and accessible with a range of exercises and activities to add interest and variety to any coaching programme. Read it, absorb it, read it again, then practise, practise, practise, to make the MAGIC happen.'
— **Jan Doyle**, Founder and CEO at UP Training & Development Ltd

'Rosie is an outstanding coach, trainer and facilitator. The book summarises all the wisdom built up over twenty years of coaching and is highly recommended for coaches old and new.'
— **Jem Stein**, Founder and CEO at The Bike Project

'Rosie Nice is well placed to provide this wonderful book, which is essential for leaders and practitioners coaching in today's business environment. She has a wealth of knowledge and experience both as a coach and a trainer of coaches. She engages the reader with her practical approaches and warm, easy to absorb tone of voice. I would highly recommend this book to anyone who seeks to develop their coaching skills and knowledge.'
— **Sara Charlesworth**, studied coaching with Rosie

'Rosie is an undisputed authority on coaching. The nurturing personality that she brings to her in-person coaching training shines through in this book. It will benefit the reader enormously, as it has benefitted me.'
— **Richard Tams**, Founder and Director, Tailwind Advisory

'I honed my own coaching skills under Rosie's expert guidance, benefitting from her years of experience as a coach and learning the models described in the book, which I have used successfully in my own coaching and consultancy business. I can thoroughly recommend this book as a guide for both new and experienced coaches.'
— **Jo Boswell**, Founder and Director, Sentio-B Ltd

'As a trainer of coaches Rosie has an extraordinary ability to land a concept so you can immediately put your learning into action. Through her training, I have directly benefited from her wisdom and experience, enabling me to shape my own practice within a solid framework and understanding of the profession. This book is a must-read for anyone embarking on a career as a coach.'
— **Jane Carne**, Business and Life Coach at Better Talk Ltd

THE MAGIC HAPPENS IN THE SILENCE

A guide to the art of reflective coaching

ROSIE NICE

Rᵉthink

First published in Great Britain in 2022
by Rethink Press (www.rethinkpress.com)

Cover image © Shutterstock | TMvectorart

Author photograph by Pennie Withers
www.penniewithersphotography.co.uk

'Silence is one of the great arts of conversation.'
Marcus Tullius Cicero

Contents

Foreword

I remember when Rosie first told me that she was writing a book. She was preparing for a learning and development session at my company, Farsight Consulting, and we were discussing how to get the best out of the team. I thought the book sounded like a great way to share her ideas and insights with a wider audience, and create something clients could take away and refer to.

I was fortunate enough to have sight of various drafts as Rosie shaped the methods and iterated the approaches, seeing the book develop over many months of hard work. We've used all the MAGIC methods in one way or another within Farsight, and I have seen first-hand the impact they can have.

Farsight works across the private and public sectors, helping organisations transform their services, think through tricky situations and solve difficult problems. Our people are crucial to our business – without smart, well-adjusted people who understand and care about what we do and why we do it, we would not be successful.

During her time with us, Rosie has seen Farsight grow from a team of 10 to over 100, and the integration of a coaching culture has been central to our success. Using the methods set out in her book, Rosie and her colleagues supported the development of our people, adding her techniques to our own. Rosie has helped us to hold up a mirror to our business, which we can use to examine the way we think, giving us the opportunity to explore our ideas and try new things. Through this process, we learn more about what we're trying to achieve and why we want to achieve it – and if we're paying attention, we learn more about ourselves.

For many years, we've used these techniques successfully within Farsight to help our people think things through, explore their motivations, develop ideas and plan their career. The techniques work just as well for personal development as professional development. I've certainly used many of them when working on my personal development and I know many of the Farsight team have too.

Rosie has brought together decades of experience into a simple structure that can work for anyone. The Farsight team and I have benefitted greatly from Rosie's guidance and thoughtful challenge, and I'm sure readers of this book will find the same.

Pete Masters
Founder and Chairman, Farsight Consulting

Introduction

I love coaching. Its powers are truly transformational, helping us to identify and achieve our hopes and dreams; it enables us to define and then become our best selves and, ultimately, to realise our full potential.

I wrote this book to share my passion, and my aim is to capture the best ideas, techniques, exercises and approaches, identified through over twenty years of being immersed in the wonderful world of learning and development. Thank you for finding this book, and I hope it inspires you to bring coaching into your life.

The subtitle of this book is 'a guide to the art of reflective coaching'. I chose these words with care, and I would like to start by explaining this definition. As a guide, it is designed to act as your companion, supporting and accompanying you on your journey to becoming a coach. By describing coaching as an art, I pay tribute to its beauty and power. The *Collins English Dictionary* definition of 'art' refers to the 'realm... of what is beautiful, appealing, or of more than ordinary significance', and this seems to me to encapsulate perfectly the essence of good coaching.

By using the term 'reflective coaching', I want to capture the central significance of the coach's role in facilitating reflection, both external and internal. External reflection is where we help the coachees examine their current situation, personal or professional; internal reflection is where we explore their capabilities and their aspirations, goals, motivations and mindsets. A skilled coach reflects a coachee's words back to them, and this enables them to develop greater self-awareness and a better understanding of themselves and their impact on others, with all the benefits this brings. You will have seen the image of a mirror on the front cover, and in the book you will become well acquainted with the use of a metaphorical mirror to facilitate reflection during coaching.

When I am helping people learn to coach, these are the concerns I hear most frequently: 'I understand that I need to ask questions as a coach, but how do I identify the best questions to ask? How can I juggle all the dynamics of a coaching conversation – building rapport, creating trust, listening without judgement, observing body language, managing the time, taking notes – and still manage to ask insightful questions?'

To help with this very real challenge, I created the five stage MAGIC Methodology around which this book is centred. Many moons ago, while both coaching professionally and training new coaches, I started to list the most effective coaching questions. I recorded everyone's favourites, collated and tested them. As a definitive list began to emerge, I grouped the questions into stages to reflect the progressive steps of a coaching process, before narrowing it down to a succinct set of what I believed to be the most effective questions, aiming to create a natural flow through the coaching process.

From this I developed the step-by-step coaching framework of the MAGIC Methodology, which we will work through together. Many people have had their views incorporated into this final version, and numerous variations have been tested in a wide variety of situations over many years. This methodology has enabled our trainee coaches to develop their emerging skills and added structure and depth to their coaching. The MAGIC Methodology can now provide you with the ultimate list of core coaching questions to give you the perfect start to your journey as a coach; from here you can go on to create your own coaching style and your own coaching magic.

The book will guide you through the five stages of the MAGIC Methodology. At each stage of the methodology, there are three carefully worded questions for you to ask your coachee, to facilitate the self-reflection which is so central to a successful coaching experience. When you first start coaching, this framework of fifteen questions can be used as your guiding star, to lead you through your sessions and keeping you on track. The framework is flexible enough to be used both within a single coaching conversation or spread over a coaching programme spanning many sessions. It begins with opening questions to start your coaching journey and leads you right the way through to the end, with closing questions to bring your coaching to a satisfying conclusion.

I will help you understand the rationale behind each question and explain why each question has been included at each stage. As you read, you will gain broader knowledge about coaching as a discipline and will also learn a range of coaching tools and techniques to add richness and variety to your coaching sessions. Each of the fifteen questions plays a crucial part in the progressive sequence but can also work perfectly alone: posed at the right time, just one well-chosen question can be transformational. All you may have to ask is, 'If you had a magic wand, what would you like to achieve?' (Question 4), or 'What has stopped you crossing this bridge already?' (Question 6) to create a moment of inspiration.

As you develop and grow as a coach, you will find your own ways of asking the questions, rewording them and making them your own. You'll develop an ability to ask insightful follow-up questions to enrich the conversation, but I hope you always remember the simple power in the overall MAGIC framework.

I have named this book *The MAGIC Happens In The Silence* because it perfectly captures the beauty of the moment. At its most fundamental level, coaching represents a simple process of asking questions and listening carefully to the responses, providing time and space to enable people to slow down, reflect and find their own answers. It is within that silence that the magic happens, and I want to share with you the key to unlocking this magic.

When we are coaching, we often find that, deep down, our coachees already know the solutions to the dilemmas they face; at some level, they know what they need to do, but they may not realise this until they are guided to examine their current situation, explore their aspirations, articulate their goals and clarify their thoughts. I know I have asked the right question when my coachee pauses and says nothing. When the room falls silent, when they look to the ceiling and they take a breath, then I stop and I wait. I wait because I know what is at play: the magic is happening in the silence.

I hope I will inspire you to incorporate coaching into your life. Even if you do not intend to formally practise as a coach, most of us could benefit from the essential coaching habits of talking a little less and listening a little more. Delegates on our coaching programmes often tell us that the skills they have learned have transformed their relationships at home as well as work. One participant credited her new skills with revitalising her relationship with her teenagers, explaining that, 'Instead of telling them what to do, I now ask questions and help them to work out their own plans for themselves.' Another spoke of how he was now having completely different conversations with his partner.

The skills of a coach are highly transferable, adding value in every aspect of our lives. I have benefited hugely from my investment in developing these skills, and I am excited to share what I have learned. If you want to harness the power of coaching for yourself, there is a section at the end discussing how to use the MAGIC Methodology to be a coach to yourself. Personally, and professionally, I am confident that this book will enable you to spread your wings and take flight, in the process enabling others to do the same.

Let's get started.

PART ONE
THE MAGIC OF COACHING

1
What Is Coaching?

First things first. A book about coaching must begin with a definition, so let us start by asking, 'What *is* coaching?'

Coaching is fundamentally about helping people to identify, define and achieve their goals, thereby learning and growing to reach their true potential. Coaching facilitates personal development and helps fulfil untapped potential. Through a supportive process which balances insightful questioning with inspiring goal planning, a good coach stimulates your thinking, creating space for the magic to happen in the silence.

I am confident that everyone, whatever your role or personal situation, can gain immediate benefits from learning essential coaching skills, even if you have no intention of becoming a professional coach. Coaching is a highly effective way to maximise potential, both in yourself and in others, and on so many occasions, I have seen coaching enable people to flourish, boosting motivation, engagement, performance and, ultimately, life satisfaction.

Within an organisational environment, coaching is increasingly being recognised as a key leadership capability and many organisations are working to create a coaching culture within their leadership teams. Upskilling a team of coaches to exemplify best practice can build beacons of excellence within an emerging coaching culture, creating a ripple effect across the organisation. A coaching culture can lead to a myriad of benefits including reduced attrition, increased engagement and loyalty.

Developing your personal coaching skills is a great way to contribute to this growing shift in leadership styles while also boosting your own career prospects. Skilled coaches are becoming a hugely valued resource, and learning to coach will help you influence, communicate and lead more effectively, enabling you to add immediate value through your enhanced capabilities. It also opens a new potential career path, either within an organisation or independently. Within my business, we meet many people who are at a career crossroads, who have left their roles in organisations to create balance in their lives, for their families or to pursue other interests, and are now seeking a way of using their skills in a new way. Coaching fits their needs perfectly. It is stimulating, interesting and challenging, and as a coach, you can develop your personal niche around your existing areas of expertise or interest.

Perhaps you already have some experience as a coach but would like to feel more confident by enhancing your practical coaching skills? I meet many people who have a degree of pre-existing understanding: some have read widely to develop a broad knowledge base, while others have completed online coaching courses and gained some form of qualification, but still lack confidence.

On one of our recent coaching programmes a delegate confessed that, although he was technically already a qualified coach, he had learned no practical skills at all during his training. He had a lot of theoretical knowledge but was uncertain that he could conduct an effective coaching conversation because he had never actually done it.

Similarly, when I completed my first coaching qualification, way back in 2003, my course was a distance learning programme with a purely academic focus. I had to write a lot of essays and post them off to be marked (the internet was just a baby back then and online learning had a long way to go!) and I managed to gain a coaching qualification without ever having properly coached anyone at all.

If you already work in a space related to learning and development, you may be finding that you are increasingly being asked to coach your clients or colleagues; if this is the case, you may feel a need to upskill yourself quickly. This was my personal motivation when I gained my first coaching qualification all those years ago. As a leadership trainer, clients who had completed a training programme frequently began to ask me for follow-up coaching. As I began to take on this work, I quickly discovered that coaching is a totally different skill to the one-to-one training I already offered. While one-to-one training is hugely valuable, it isn't coaching. I needed to learn the difference, and fast.

Coaching is a practical skill – it is all about the *doing* not just the *knowing*. This book has therefore deliberately been written as a practical guide, encouraging you to practise and enhance your developing skills. It's not enough just to know about coaching, you must be able to do it too. In this book I will provide a guide for your coaching sessions and clearly explain the rationale for the questions that you are asking, and I will encourage you to practise, practise, practise.

In summary, I truly believe that learning to coach can bring wonderful benefits in whichever context you choose to use your skills. Whether you are looking to enhance your career prospects, seeking a new role or more flexible working, considering a career change or self-employment, or even if you would simply like to engage at a deeper level with friends, family, colleagues or team members, learning to coach can add value to your life. This book is the perfect place to start your coaching journey.

Past, present and future selves

When considering coaching, I think a great way to think about it is in terms of the three versions of the self – past, present and future. Consider these questions:

- Who am I?

- Who are you?

- Are we the same people we were when we were children?

- Will we be the same person we are now in five, ten or twenty years' time?

Big questions indeed, and ones I love to contemplate accompanied by a glass of wine and a beautiful sunset!

One of my favourite sayings, often used in our household, is 'Be a friend to your future self.' I love this concept of our past, present and future selves. Our present selves are all living with the consequences of decisions made by our past selves, sometimes years ago, and choices made now by our present selves may have far reaching effects on our future selves. Coaching is about harnessing this concept and proactively taking control of the choices we make now which will impact these future versions of ourselves.

I have a strong independent streak within me, and sometimes I just want to do exactly what I feel like doing right now. However, when I plan ahead – complete a piece of work well before a deadline, put away a little money each month for a rainy day, or even do a weekly meal plan on a Sunday – I secretly feel beautifully self-congratulatory, remembering that I am being a friend to my future self. When I then approach the deadline in a calm state, have funds for an unexpected bill or have the ingredients to cook a mid-week dinner, I thank my past version who looked ahead and invested time and effort to make life easier for my present self.

With coaching, you can learn how best 'present you' can make investments of energy and effort now to support the 'future you'. When time moves on, as it inevitably does, and the 'future you' has become you now, you will feel a rush of gratitude towards the 'past you' that got you here.

EXERCISE: Past me, present me and future me

Here's a great exercise to try, on your own or guiding a coachee, to demonstrate this powerful concept. You don't have to do it physically – it works just as well if you do it digitally, but sometimes an element of movement can add extra dynamism to our coaching.

Take three real/virtual sheets of paper, and on the first page write 'Past Me', the second page, 'Present Me', and 'Future Me' on the last, then place them side-by-side.

Past Me	Present Me	Future Me

Begin by thinking of a pivotal moment when the past you made a decision for which the present you is eternally grateful: a sacrifice you made, a change you embraced or a risk you took which is bringing benefits to you now.

Turn first to the sheet which represents the past you and think back to that moment. Take time to remember what it felt like at the time and how you motivated yourself to make that choice or take that action. Thank that earlier version of yourself for the foresight, determination and consideration which is now benefiting the present you. Sometimes we may be thanking ourselves for things we didn't do, when we exercised great self-control or narrowly avoided disaster, and there will also be times when we made mistakes from which we then learned, so you could think of these examples too.

Now move on to the paper representing the future you. Pick a date or an age and take a moment to inhabit that new time. How does it feel? What are you doing, thinking and feeling and how are you living? How do you want this future you to think, feel and be? Stop and really visualise this future version of yourself.

Then move back to the central paper, representing the present you. What can the present you do right now to invest in these plans you visualised and support the future you?

Let's take an example: you may currently be eating reasonably well but not doing much exercise. That may be fine for the present you, but are you doing enough to keep the 'you' of the future healthy and well? When my husband and I are finding it hard to drag ourselves off the sofa and do some exercise, we sometimes laugh and say that we will thank ourselves one day, even though it is the last thing we feel like doing right now. In the evening I always thank my earlier self for exercising in the morning, and I am sure that Old Lady Rosie will be grateful.

This visualisation exercise can help you, and your coachees, stay motivated and engaged when the going gets tough. Life may always be busy and there may always be distractions. Visualising the 'you' of the future, whether that is a day, a week, a month or even years later, saying 'thank you' to the you of the present helps us resist temptations and avoid distractions; remembering how you are investing in your future can really help you, in the present, stay focused on your aspirations and goals.

In summary, think of it like this: coaching helps the coachee be a friend to their future self.

The roles and responsibilities of a coach

Let's think now in a little more detail about what a coach actually does.

The fundamental role of a coach is to guide and support their coachee in achieving their aspirations and goals. The coach leads the process and provides the environment within which the coachee can develop the confidence to explore opportunities and generate innovative solutions, safe in the knowledge that the conversation is non-judgemental and confidential. The best ideas come from the coachee, and the best coaches encourage ownership and accountability, facilitating the process of their coachee finding their own path.

This can be challenging, particularly if you have a wider skills and knowledge base than your coachee. One of the first things I teach new coaches is to resist the temptation to tell people what to do. Our role is to increase the self-awareness of our coachee and encourage a strong sense of personal responsibility. We want our coachees to develop a sense of self-reliance and increase their ability to achieve success, whatever this means to them.

A good coach will hold up a metaphorical mirror to enable their coachees to see themselves more clearly. This enables your coachee to develop several key skills:

- Reflect on their current situation so they learn to know themselves better, understand their personal values, their strengths and development areas, and examining their personal circumstances, analyse what is working well and what is not working so well.

- Explore their aspirations and clearly define their goals, enabling them to better visualise their ideal future.

- Understand where they are now in relation to those goals and identify any barriers that currently stand in the way of achieving success.

- Work through ideas and potential pathways for achieving these goals.

- Create a plan to move forwards, identifying milestones and timescales and make commitments to carry out clear and specific actions.

As coaches, we guide our coachee through a structured process to help them articulate goals and create a plan, and then we support them as they work to achieve these goals. We help them develop greater self-awareness by asking probing, reflective questions which encourage them to re-examine their own feelings, thoughts and behaviours.

Being a coach carries a significant weight of obligation and accountability. We have a responsibility to always act ethically and to follow the law, respecting diversity and inclusion, being non-judgemental in our approach, maintaining confidentiality and always acting fairly and equitably. It is also our duty to prioritise the well-being of our coachee and to ensure a safe environment, honouring our duty of care.

We have a responsibility to demonstrate and maintain high standards and continuously invest in our own professional development, refreshing our skills and keeping our knowledge current and up to date. It is best practice for us personally to engage in coaching or supervision, to help us reflect on our capabilities and support us through any stressful issues which might jeopardise our professional objectivity. Engaging in reflective practice is an effective way to develop and improve our coaching skills by examining what went well and what we could have done differently after every coaching session, accelerating our personal development.

We also have a responsibility to recognise when coaching isn't the answer and when another form of intervention will serve our coachee better. Sometimes training, mentoring, or even giving direct instructions is the best way to help others develop, grow and achieve success. We are going to address this later and consider how and when we should swap our coaching role for another, equally valid way of offering support. We must always remain committed to our fundamental obligation as a coach: to support our coachees in moving out of the zone of what they know, towards the zone of their full potential.

Leaving the zone of the known

What words come to mind when you think of the concept of home? Safety, security and comfort spring to mind for me. Although the reality may be different, the idealised thought of home leaves me feeling warm and cocooned. It is what I call the 'zone of the known', – the zone of our present selves. This is a lovely place to imagine, but it is not a place where we stretch ourselves. When we truly want to develop and grow, we need to consciously step out of this cocoon of familiarity into the zone of the unknown, the zone of our potential and our future selves. When we choose to make this step, we move into the place where learning happens, but its position is outside what you know and therefore is a challenging place to be.

As coaches, it is our job to supportively challenge our coachees by taking them into this zone of their potential, to question their existing beliefs and behaviours and explore new ones. The concept of exploring can feel exciting but also a bit daunting, so we must be careful not to push coachees too far over their limits where they can tip over into feeling lost and scared. If we misjudge a situation and people feel over-challenged, the typical reaction is to speedily retreat to the safety of home and the security of the zone of the known. The opportunity for learning and growth is lost, along with trust.

For all of us, facing our fears and stepping out of the zone of the known requires support, encouragement, and above all, trust.

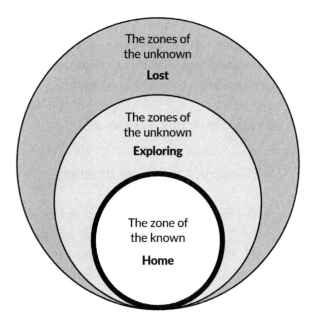

Here is a personal story which demonstrates the importance of a good balance between the key elements necessary for growth, support and challenge and that led me to three interesting insights which I later applied back at work.

On a recent summer holiday, my husband and I had the fantastic pleasure of a cheeky few days away on a Mediterranean island. With a great deal of trepidation, we bravely signed up for a guided sea swim around a nearby island. It was well outside our known zone, and we'd never done anything like this before, but it sounded fun and the risk-loving side of me was asking myself, 'What could possibly go wrong?' The activity began with a short talk and a few tips, and then we leaped in and embarked on our group swim along the spectacular Croatian coastline. The leaders were encouraging and enthusiastic throughout, and it was an amazing experience. It was hard but we loved the adventure.

What did I learn from this experience?

Everyone's zones are different

When we had finished, the first question our instructor asked was, 'Who felt that they were stepping into the unknown during the swim?' It was a good question and led to an interesting discussion. We were all willing volunteers who had chosen to join this activity but still, there was a wide range of responses: several people felt delighted that they had explored the limits of what they could do, while others could have gone further and faster.

A great sense of satisfaction and achievement can be felt when we move away from the psychological safety of what we know, into the unknown zones of our potential, but the key is to recognise that everyone's zones are different. The outer edges of the unknown can be a scary place, and great empathy is required when others struggle with something which we find easy. Our swimming guides managed this well, demonstrating warmth and humour and reassuring us with their confidence, but without intimidating us with their own huge confidence levels as experienced and confident sea swimmers.

Learning happens outside the zone of the known

The adventure swim pushed many of us well into new territory. We supported and encouraged each other, spurring others on and felt a great sense of collective achievement. Everyone gave a huge round of applause, for ourselves and for each other, as we emerged from the water having swum 2,000 metres round the island.

This adventure stretched me and pushed me well into exploring the zone of the unknown. Experiences which help us step outside the zone of the known can enable us to achieve far more than we thought possible, and this spectacular experience has stayed with me. While I hugely enjoyed the swimming element of the day and gladly pushed myself to explore my capabilities to gain the most from the challenge, we fast reached my personal limits when the session finished with the cheery, 'Let's all jump off the jetty one by one, while we film you!' I had challenged myself enough for one day. Social media plus me in a bikini pushes me over my personal limits, and I rapidly disappeared out of shot!

Exploring our limits on holiday can give us courage back at home

When you regularly push yourself, your courage is rewarded as your personal known zone expands and your unknown zone pushes further away. I am no adrenaline junkie – far from it – but confidence gained from activities like this wild swimming adventure undoubtedly helps when I face challenges at home and work. Several times since, when I have found myself feeling nervous, I've reassured myself, 'You swam two kilometres in the open sea; you can do this!'

EXERCISE: List your personal triumphs

Since this swim, I have often drawn on the experience in my coaching. It clearly demonstrated to me how important it is, in our roles as coaches, to tune in to people's known and unknown zones, to help them develop and achieve their best.

A great exercise to do right now would be to write down a list of things you have done that stretched and pushed you and which make you proud. It might be a physical challenge like my swim, an academic achievement like an exam, a performance, a presentation or even having an uncomfortable conversation or overcoming a personal fear.

What did you learn from these achievements?

Can you think of occasions where you have drawn strength from the courage demonstrated at the time?

If your list is currently a little short, are there things you could do in the future to stretch and grow your known zone?

When I consider my own list, apart from this sea swim, one of my key personal triumphs is learning to cope with a terrible fear of spiders. In honour of me progressing from becoming a total wreck if I see anything with eight legs to now being able to take deep breaths and slowly leave the room (this is still a work in progress!), my husband bought me a mug with a beautifully worded inscription: 'No longer does she fear the spider. Instead, she draws strength from the knowledge of her bravery in its presence.' Thank you to Edward Monkton for summing my achievement up quite perfectly.

It's scary for all of us to leave the psychological safety of the zone of the known, and sometimes we need to dig really deep to keep going but, with support, trust and encouragement, we can really surprise ourselves.

When coaching isn't the answer

You have probably gathered by now that I think coaching is wonderful. It can release potential, realise aspirations, create ideas, harness creativity, unlock potential and help overcome obstacles, both internal and external.

When I am coaching, I will often say to my coachee, 'I am going to be asking you lots of questions; this isn't an exam, and there are no right or wrong answers. This is about helping you to reflect and think clearly.' I also make sure the coachee understands that they can change their answers at any time. Sometimes people begin to reply and then stop, pause and immediately correct themselves: 'Actually, I don't think that at all.' That's great and I love it when that happens because it means that as soon as they articulate even a long-held belief or thought, they are now beginning to question it; often they then realise that is isn't, or is no longer, what they actually believe after all. The magic has happened in the silence.

Having established the unquestionable benefits of coaching, we must also remember that there are some instances where coaching may not be the answer. Our coachee's ability to come up with their own answers and effectively help themselves is fundamentally dependent on their levels of knowledge, experience, skill, confidence, motivation, commitment and enthusiasm. If one or more of these levels are low, our questions may be met with silence or even confusion. They may struggle or even refuse to find any appropriate responses or be unclear how and why they should be engaging with you. Sometimes their only response might be, 'I just don't know. I have never done this before', and they may just become frustrated with the conversation or with themselves.

Let us consider why this is. As an example, remember when you last went through the process of learning to use new technology or software. It would be enormously frustrating and even demoralising to be asked specific questions such as 'How do you think you could populate this spreadsheet?' or 'How would you operate this equipment?' if you have never seen anything like it before. It is much more efficient if someone first teaches you what to do, before then asking you to demonstrate your understanding. Where you need to learn a new skill, coaching is not the answer. It is training or teaching that you need, albeit perhaps using a coaching style which helps you learn by asking questions and encouraging participation.

Another occasion when coaching would be totally inappropriate would be in an emergency. It would be positively dangerous for a manager to ask, 'What do you think our evacuation procedures should be?' while chaos reigned all around. In the heat of the moment, a direct and unambiguous approach is required, along the lines of 'Evacuate the building now!' If this discussion is taking place before or after such an event, however, asking, 'How are we going to ensure we are well placed to deal with an emergency?' would be a great coaching question to help a health and safety manager think through their strategies and plans.

As a coach, you don't have to be an expert in the subject matter of the coaching because coaching is itself a skill; in-depth knowledge of a subject can sometimes even get in the way of coaching because it can become so difficult not simply to tell people what to do. You may have been hired as an independent coach specifically because of your knowledge and experience, and people will then be frustrated if you don't then share your skills and expertise. There will be moments when you will have more knowledge and experience than your coachee, and you may be able to provide a solution that no amount of coaching is going to help your coachee reach, so on these occasions, proposing a solution may be appropriate.

While there is nothing wrong with offering advice and suggesting solutions and at times it can be hugely helpful, it is important to be aware that when doing this you are not practising coaching. This approach is more akin to training, teaching or mentoring. Each of these have their own valuable part to play, but they are different to coaching. In such situations, it can be helpful and wholly appropriate for you to step out of the role of coach and instead put on a different hat. Possible alternatives include:

- A leader offering strategic direction

- A consultant or expert offering solutions

- A mentor offering advice

- A skills-development trainer

- A counsellor (this is a hat to wear with caution, passing to a professional where necessary)

The key here is your own self-awareness, recognising when you are moving from one role to another and doing so mindfully, because you have decided that this is the right approach at this time, for this person, in this situation.

Remember that if we identify a skill or knowledge gap which is affecting performance, coaching may not be the best way to bridge this gap. Teaching the required skills may be faster, more efficient and ultimately more successful, and so may simply telling people what to do. However, coaching *can* be the most effective solution when the primary obstacle to success is not a gap in skills and knowledge, but something else entirely: perhaps a pattern of thinking, or a mindset, a 'limiting belief'.

Limiting beliefs can take the form of stories we tell ourselves which hold us back: 'I can't do that,' 'That won't work,' 'Other people are better than I am,' and so on. Skills-development training courses will be of limited value if what is really holding a person back is their inner critic or a fixed mindset, which coaching could easily and effectively change. In these situations, your role as coach is to create space, time and support to help your coachee figure out their answers for themselves, adopting what we call a 'coaching mindset'.

What is a coaching mindset?

A coaching mindset develops and maintains the belief that our coachee has all the answers they need within them, and it is the coach's role to help them to help themselves. It means that we approach our coaching conversations with the attitude and assumption that our coachee already possesses the internal resources they need to find their own solutions, with our support.

If you imagine a conventional social conversation being like a beam of light, moving back and forth as each person speaks, a coaching conversation keeps the beam fixed predominately upon the coachee. This is harder than it sounds. According to Thesaurus.com, 'I' is the most commonly used singular personal pronoun, showing how we all individually enjoy being lit up by this beam of light. In good coaching, if a coach decides to temporarily turn the light upon themselves and share a personal thought or experience, this is done as a mindful act designed to illuminate an issue when they feel some self-disclosure would help move the conversation forward.

A true coaching mindset necessitates us being as open-minded and non-judgemental as possible, and there has been a big increase in awareness over recent years of the influence of what is known as 'unconscious bias' as defined in *Collins English Dictionary*: 'Unconscious favouritism towards or prejudice against people of a particular ethnicity, gender, or social group that influences one's actions or perceptions.' As coaches, we need to become aware of our own inherent and subconscious biases by purposely raising them into our consciousness. There they can be challenged and sometimes deliberately rejected or set aside; more often, they cannot be entirely eradicated, but with an awareness of their presence, we can intentionally and mindfully work to minimise the impact they have on the service we provide to our clients. This can sometimes require great self-awareness and effort, and it is a process that may feel uncomfortable at times as you push yourself into the exploring zone and challenge yourself to think differently.

Here's a great example of a coaching mindset in practice, where an underlying belief in the potential of the coachee is clearly evident. It shows how a coaching approach can be used in a wide range of everyday scenarios.

When my daughter was learning to drive. I noticed that she was progressing well and learning fast. I also noticed that when her driving instructor picked her up and dropped her off, she and the instructor always spent five or ten minutes chatting in the car, so I asked her what they talked about. I was so impressed by what I heard. When the lesson started, they always spent a few minutes recapping what she had learned last time. Between each lesson, she was set a specific task to practise and the instructor began every lesson by asking how the task had gone and reviewing her progress. Each lesson had a specific objective – perhaps mastering roundabouts, parking or dual carriageways. When they were driving, if my daughter made a mistake, the instructor would ask her to pull over and stop so they could have a chat. 'What just happened?' he would ask, inviting my daughter to review her performance. The instructor would then add his feedback, making sure that my daughter knew what to do next time, and off they would go again. At the end of each lesson, he would ask my daughter what she had learned, recap the key takeaway points and set the task to practise for the next lesson. This is a fantastic example of a coaching mindset in practice and shows how brilliantly it can be applied in any situation. Her instructor was perfectly balancing the role of teacher and coach, to great effect.

We have covered a lot of ground in Part One. We've learned that adopting a coaching mindset is a simple and powerful way to transform your conversations and your relationships, and we've talked about the life-changing benefits coaching can bring, for you and for your coachees, as you learn the art of inspirational, reflective coaching. We've discussed the role of a coach, and the importance of developing a coaching mindset. Now it's time to introduce the coaching model that's central to this book: the MAGIC Methodology.

PART TWO
THE MAGIC
METHODOLOGY

2
Why Use A Methodology?

This is a good question. The answer in my view is simple: a good coaching methodology provides an invaluable guide, a road map for you to follow in your coaching practice. Particularly when you first start coaching, using a methodology to structure your sessions is a powerful way to develop your capability and your confidence.

The MAGIC Methodology aims to provide you with a clear framework for your coaching. It can be used within one self-contained coaching session or across a multisession coaching programme, and it is accompanied by a carefully selected series of questions for use as you systematically move through the coaching process. It has been designed to be applicable in a wide range of situations, creating the perfect balance between structure and flexibility so that you can adapt it in response to the needs of each coachee. It works as well in an organisational setting, where managers are coaching their teams, as it does in a consultancy setting where independent coaches are working with autonomous individuals.

The five stages of the MAGIC Methodology

The MAGIC Methodology leads you through five distinct stages of a coaching process. It represents a cyclical process and can be used to structure each coaching session, starting by analysing where our coachee is now, enabling them to assess their current situation, its strengths and its drawbacks. We then work with them to share their aspirations, define clear goals and help them map the process by which they will achieve success. The framework culminates with a clear plan, and then the whole process can potentially be used to cycle round and start again. On this occasion, you can hold your coachee accountable for taking the steps that they previously agreed and discuss their progress, before focusing on a new set of goals and actions to maintain their momentum.

We will start with an overview of the MAGIC Methodology and the purpose of each stage. We'll then delve deeper, identifying questions to ask at each stage, and looking at a range of exercises to add energy, depth and variety to your sessions.

The five stages to the methodology give us the acronym **MAGIC**:

Mirror
Aspirations
Goals
Ideas
Commitment

As we progress through the stages, it may help to think of a coaching conversation as a simple arc or a bridge, helping us move across the gap between our current situation towards a new destination.

I love the metaphor of coaching as a bridge. Bridges represent an opportunity to travel to new areas. They are built for communication, progression and travel, creating freedom of movement for those who wish to cross. A bridge makes it possible to overcome obstacles and barriers, creating a safe connection to places otherwise unknown and inaccessible.

We start by asking questions designed to help us begin our journey across the bridge to our destination. We broaden out the conversation with questions designed to widen thinking and stimulate insight and reflection, moving us forward until we are standing at the top of the bridge, and can now fully visualise our goals and survey our final destination. We then move on down the other side, towards the end of our journey, gradually narrowing the conversation once again, with focused questions to formulate a specific plan of action.

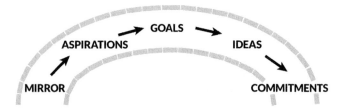

Mirror

The MAGIC Methodology begins with reflection. Once we have opened our coaching session and helped our coachee feel comfortable, the process starts by inviting them to look into a metaphorical mirror and asking, 'When you look in the mirror, what do you see?' The metaphor of the mirror facilitates the process of self-reflection, encouraging the coachee to undertake an honest and unfiltered evaluation of their current situation.

Through a series of exercises and discussions, we inspire reflection and increase self-awareness. We examine elements of their life in turn, establishing what is going well, and what not so well, what they would like to maintain and what they might choose to change; this can be applied to their regular routines, their current priorities, their ambitions, in their professional and/or personal life. This can be truly illuminating, illustrating key priorities and beliefs, revealing new convictions and understandings, and sometimes uncovering buried truths; it can, at times, be emotional, powerful, exciting and even cathartic, but it may be upsetting or provoke difficult acknowledgements or realisations. We therefore need to approach all this with sensitivity, care and empathy.

Those people who already have relatively high levels of self-awareness find this stage reasonably easy. They may have already gone through a self-evaluation process which was perhaps what motivated them to seek coaching in the first place. They may also have a sense of dissatisfaction which they are seeking to resolve, hoping coaching will help them. Others will find this harder, especially if they have never analysed themselves or their situation in this way before. I will share a series of questions, exercises and activities to help you steer though this vital stage with a careful balance of structure and flexibility, to enable a useful and rewarding discussion and set you up for success going forward.

Aspirations

We then move on, rising up the arc, as we help our coachee explore their aspirations and articulate a vision of their future. What do they want to see when they look in that mirror? What would they like to happen in the future? What would they love to achieve, personally or professionally? How do they want to feel? This can apply to a work-related assignment, a career move, a relationship dilemma or a complete life change.

We walk them through a process to help analyse where they are now in relation to that aspiration, discussing the length of the journey that they must undertake to get there.

Goals

At the top of the arc, we now gain a clearer view of what lies ahead. The bridge has elevated us so that we can see our future laid before us, and this next stage enables us to help turn those aspirations into specific and tangible goals based on their vision of the future, what they would like to achieve, by when, and why.

Ideas

Now that we have articulated the what, why and when, we turn to the how.

At the ideas stage, we continue across the bridge, drawing ever closer to the other side. Here our questions should be broad and open: 'How *could* you achieve this goal?' We are aiming to stimulate original and unencumbered thought as our coachee now generates an extensive range of ideas for how they could turn their goals into reality. As coaches, we need to avoid 'fixing the problem' or leading them towards what we consider to be best. We must step right back at this moment: it is essential that we focus on their ideas, their options and their plan; our role is to facilitate, not to lead.

Commitments

This final stage deals with commitments, directly addressing the question 'How will you achieve this goal?' At this stage, those on the bridge are nearing the ground once again, but now on the other side. Your coachee has been informed and inspired by their journey across the bridge, and now you help them develop their best ideas into a workable and effective plan, firing them up to create momentum and take action.

Effective coaching is a cyclical process. We may need to cross the bridge many times, as we now need to review progress regularly, set new goals and milestones and create a system of continuous improvement, celebrating every small step forward to motivate our coachees to keep on going, even when the going gets tough.

Key principles

As we move now to examine the MAGIC Methodology in more detail, there are three key principles which are central to its successful application:

1. Ask, don't tell.

2. Listen more than you talk.

3. Create silence and space for the magic to happen.

Ask, don't tell

Anyone who has trained as a coach will recognise this as one of the first principles we learn, and one of the most difficult to apply. Managers in the workplace can find it especially hard to stop giving instructions; as a manager, you are expected to have the answers – surely that's your role? It is easy to find yourself telling people what they should do, and often how they should do it. It's quicker, simpler and you're far more likely to get things done when and as you want them done, but how much real engagement does this create, and how stressful will it feel to be considered the font of all knowledge?

Consider what would happen if, instead of stating 'This is what I think,' you instead tried asking, 'What do you think?' Changing your approach in this way frees up your time, releases the potential of your people and can reduce the parent-child nature of many manager/team relationships; it's win-win-win. Give them the space and stand back: if the teams can successfully generate their own actions and plans, then that's great; if they aren't able to do so, then you know you have a skills or confidence gap that you need to address, perhaps through training or mentoring.

Listen more than you talk

This is a good principle for life, not just for coaching. One tip I remember learning early in my training career is that we have two ears and one mouth, and we should use them in those proportions. The role of a coach is to really listen: to hear what is being said, and also what is not; to listen to the way things are being said, to the tone of voice and the choice of vocabulary; and to pay attention to the underlying subtext and the visual message of the body language. We can only do this when we bring our whole selves to a coaching conversation, when we really show up and are truly present, able to ignore the chatter in our heads.

Create silence and space for the magic to happen

If we move through our coaching questions too rapidly, our coachee will reply with the answers they already know and thoughts they have already had. If we slow down and allow time to pause and reflect, we create space for the magic to happen in the silence between your questions, while your coachee pauses for thought.

It happens when you ask a question and wait, holding the space and resisting the temptation to interrupt or, even worse, to answer the question yourself.

The silence also happens between your sessions. One of the wonders of coaching is that the transformative effect on your coachee isn't just confined to your sessions together: the true value comes before, after and between the sessions. They will be thinking about the coaching on the way to your sessions and contemplating your discussions afterwards; also when they are diligently completing their actions and doing their homework – we hope! It is in this thoughtful space and silence that the magic is happening. It happens even in the silence when you haven't heard from your coachee. They may be thinking about your sessions in the shower, when they're idly looking out of the window, or when driving, exercising, gardening… and probably when they should be concentrating in a meeting.

Here is a personal example. I recently underwent a programme of coaching sessions with a colleague who was working towards a coaching qualification and needed some practice. I was delighted to help. It was great to be able to talk for an hour about my goals and aspirations, and I came away each time fired up and full of enthusiasm. What I then began to realise was how much additional value I was gaining outside the sessions we had together. I thought about it all the way there and all the way home. I thought about it when I was planning my week or cooking the supper.

I thought about it the day before our session when I was frantically trying to complete the actions to which I had committed because I knew that she would ask me about them. Several times I unexpectedly had what I call a 'lightbulb moment', when my subconscious was clearly working hard even while I was outwardly engaged in other activities. This so clearly demonstrated to me how much magic was happening in the silence between the sessions.

Coaching questions

The questions in our MAGIC questioning arc have been carefully worded to encourage introspection and reflection, without feeling like an interrogation. The questions we ask, and the way we phrase them, are crucially important, but in my experience, too often coaching sessions will focus narrowly in on 'What do you want to achieve?' and 'How are you going to do to achieve it?' That is useful, up to a point, because you are helping a coachee to clarify goals and create an action plan, but that isn't magic.

The questions asked by the best coaches create moments of true clarity where a coachee realises something which they had never appreciated before. The more coaching I do, the more I understand that it is not the simpler task-focused *what* questions, but the more probing *why* questions that enable the greatest self-realisation and those 'light bulb' moments which create the magic.

'Why' questions stimulate what educationalists call 'higher-order thinking'. This means moving beyond a basic assessment of facts, information and simple action plans towards the use of more in-depth skills such as evaluation, analysis, sophisticated problem solving and greater creativity. You may have heard these types of questions described as 'powerful'; I like to think of our fifteen questions as beautiful, and they are also magical. They are certainly designed to act as a catalyst for change.

To help us better understand what makes a question 'powerful', 'beautiful' or 'magic', we can think of a hierarchy of questions, depicted on a pyramid. Fact-based, closed questions sit at the bottom, where they are used to establish facts and gain information, and powerful, insightful, probing questions sit at the top, where they are used to inspire higher-order thinking. Both question types are useful and both have their place; the real skill lies in knowing when, and why, we ask each type of question.

It takes time to build trust and gain permission to ask powerful, probing questions that inspire higher-order thinking; if not first obtained, these searching questions can seem intrusive and can damage our coaching relationships. We need to create a safe, non-judgemental environment to gain consent to ask these deeper and more personal questions, and thus enable our coaching to reap meaningful rewards.

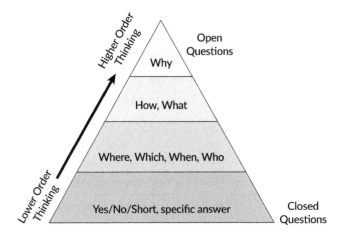

Before we move on, here is a final model to help you create the all-important **SILENCE** in your coaching, to enable the magic to happen.

Slow down:	Don't rush the process, create space and time.
Introspection:	Create opportunities for reflective thought.
Listen:	Listen to what people are really saying as well as what they are not.
Empathy:	Understand their perspective and put yourself in their shoes.
Notice:	Pay attention to non-verbal cues, tone of voice and body language.
Calm:	Create a calm, supportive and non-judgemental environment.
Engage:	Minimise external distractions and be fully present throughout.

The MAGIC questioning arc

At the heart of the MAGIC Methodology are fifteen core coaching questions, creating a flow to guide you through the process. These questions form the backbone of inspirational coaching and the essence of this book.

Holding up a mirror to reflect on your current situation

1	Mirror	What can you tell me about your current situation?
2	Mirror	What would you like to focus on?
3	Mirror	What makes this important to you now?

Articulating your aspirations

4	Aspirations	If you had a magic wand, what would you like to achieve?
5	Aspirations	How would you describe the bridge you will need to cross to achieve this aspiration?
6	Aspirations	What has stopped you crossing this bridge before now?

Turning these aspirations into specific goals

7	Goals	Can you create a clear goal, achievable within a realistic timeframe?
8	Goals	Can you identify some milestones to mark your progress along the way?
9	Goals	To focus on this goal, what else might you need to set aside?

Generating ideas		
10	Ideas	What ideas do you have for how to achieve this goal?
11	Ideas	Where could you go for help, advice, support and inspiration?
12	Ideas	How can you evaluate these ideas?
Creating a plan and making commitments		
13	Commitments	What's your plan?
14	Commitments	What is the first thing you will do to start you on your way?
15	Commitments	What are your biggest takeaways from today's session?

We'll now look at each question in detail, enhancing the discussion with a wide range of exercises for you to use to ensure your coaching sessions are truly reflective, engaging, varied, insightful and motivating.

3
Question 1 (Mirror)
What can you tell me about your current situation?

How we open our sessions is critically important as this sets the tone for your entire coaching relationship. Every coaching session and programme should have a clear opening and an effective close, and the MAGIC questioning arc fits neatly within this structure.

Whether this is your first session together or a follow-on from a previous meeting, a coaching session should always open with a welcome and a check-in to see how the coachee is – 'What can you tell me about your current situation?' This is a gentle and unthreatening opening to set the scene for an interactive discussion and encourage your coachee to begin to talk, preparing them look into a metaphorical mirror, see their own life in reflection and consider where they are right now.

A key part of our role as coaches is to help our coachees articulate their goals, defining and clarifying them and painting a picture of their wonderful world of success. Many coaching models reflect this by recommending that you start by asking your coachee to describe their goals, with a question like, 'What do you want to achieve?' I disagree. I frequently find that my coachees don't actually know what their goals are when we first start talking. If I ask them straight away what they want to achieve, then I am often met with confusion, a shrug or a blank look; 'I don't know,' they say, 'That's why I am here.' People often seek coaching because they are feeling dissatisfied or they are stuck, and they don't quite know why, or what to do next. What they really need to discuss is where they are right now; they can't envisage where they want to be in the future until they make sense of the present. They may know that something isn't right and that they want to make changes, they may even be clear about what they *don't* want, but often they don't know what they *do* want. They may have the motivation, but their ability to make changes for the future only really comes after they have gained a true understanding of the present.

Throughout many years of coaching, I've found that usually what people need to begin with is a discussion about where they are now. They want to talk about what they are struggling with and their current issues. They want me to get to know them and come to understand their individual personal circumstances and their unique set of challenges and achievements. They want to feel heard and understood, and only then will they start to open up about their hopes and aspirations for the future.

There are many alternative ways to phrase this opening question:

- How are you?
- How are you feeling?
- What's happening at the moment?
- What is currently taking up your emotional energy?
- How is business?
- How is your project going?

However you phrase it, the question presents a perfect opportunity for your coachee to begin by offloading. It's not uncommon for them to just decompress and simply tell you what is on their mind. Part of the initial rapport and relationship building within coaching stems from showing that you are interested and that you recognise people's need to be listened to. This opening question allows people to share what is at the forefront of their mind, eradicating some of the noise of their immediate thoughts. Sometimes you will see people physically sigh with relief when they have begun this process of removing some of their mental clutter; it feels like releasing the pressure of an over-inflated balloon.

Here's a personal example. Several years ago, I was involved in a fantastic coaching project for a global organisation. I remember arranging the first coaching call with a previous trainee, a friendly and enthusiastic sales manager. At the start, I assured her that everything we discussed was confidential and that she could speak freely and openly. She appreciated being able to talk unguardedly to someone who knew and understood the business but was not a colleague, who was objective and detached while still knowledgeable about the organisation.

'So,' I began, 'tell me about your current situation...' She talked, and she talked, and she talked, about her challenges and her difficulties, her achievements and her struggles, the people in her team and her manager, her customers and her colleagues.

'Oh,' I said, 'ah... I see... *Mm*, yes... ok... and then...?'

Before we knew it, the hour was nearly up.

'Thank you so much,' she said. 'That was amazing. I feel so much better. There is no way I can talk like this to anyone inside the organisation, so it's wonderful to be able to get my thoughts out of my head and talk them through. It's like a load has been lifted.'

My initial thought was 'Wow!' I felt I had done little except listen. It reinforced the power of really listening in a mindful and non-judgemental way, giving people space to talk.

At our next session, we moved on to look more specifically at issues she wanted to explore, going through the key learning from a training programme she had recently attended and considering how she could apply the concepts within her team. It was a productive session, but this could not have been achieved without first allowing her the opportunity to offload at the start of the first session. Our discussion was far deeper because we had already established a strong and open relationship based on trust and confidentiality, enabling her to share her thoughts and feelings freely and unguardedly.

We do need to be careful about how we phrase this opening question, however. One man on a recent coaching course, a successful retail manager who travelled round his stores coaching and motivating his sales consultants, shared a common dilemma with his fellow participants:

'I know I need to ask questions and listen, without interrupting, but I only have a limited time in each store. Sometimes when I arrive and ask how they are, they spend so long telling me about their broken washing machine and their partner's bad back that we run out of time, and I am left with no opportunity to do any work-related coaching.'

All the delegates nodded in recognition at this story. It is a true challenge to keep the conversation on track when we have a coachee who likes to talk!

We talked it through to help him see another way to approach this situation. Remembering a key coaching attribute, I resisted the strong temptation to tell him what to do – we do aim to practise what we preach! Instead I asked him what else he could do, to keep the conversation on track, while still demonstrating good questioning and listening behaviours, and we gathered ideas from the group. As they debated his situation, he soon began to understand that it was the vague and open wording of his questions that was causing the difficulties. His colleagues suggested that he introduce themes to his visits, so sometimes he would focus specifically on team issues, marketing campaigns or his team's personal development. He also resolved to ask more tailored questions: 'How's business today?', 'What's happening in the store at the moment?' or 'What are currently the key issues?' The delegates quickly proposed a whole range of open questions which kept the conversation focused on business and team performance, but still demon-strated care and commitment.

When I saw him again at a subsequent workshop, he was delighted to report that this change of approach had revolutionised his working practice, enabling more structured discussions, more focused coaching sessions, higher productivity and better business results.

As these examples demonstrate, our challenge is to build an environment of trust and rapport that enables our coachee to feel heard and understood, while managing the time so we don't allow the whole session to disappear down a proverbial rabbit hole. Coaching is about goals and results – this is one of the many things which distinguishes a coaching conversation from a nice supportive chat – and it is our job to steer it naturally through the process without feeling contrived or strained. If we allow the process to go too far off adrift and don't eventually achieve a satisfactory conclusion, our coachee may feel disappointed, short changed or frustrated that it has not been a good use of their valuable time.

This MAGIC Methodology acts as your coaching sat nav; you are free to take a diversion, but it is there if you find that your session has gone off track. Life – and coaching – is never as linear we would like: life goes up and down, round and round, and so does coaching. We have new ideas and we change our minds, we say one thing and contradict ourselves two minutes later; that's life, and it happens in coaching too. You may find your coaching veers off on various detours along the way, but the MAGIC Methodology will help you find your bearings and enable you to get back on track, steering you towards the creation of a robust plan which becomes the road map towards their destination.

Our goal with this opening question is to get our coaching off to a great start, building trust and rapport, creating engagement and openness, and demonstrating empathy. We ask, 'What can you tell me about your current situation?' and we then sit back and listen. This first question is also important because we need to consider the bigger picture and understand it in context if we are to help our coachee focus on change and self-development. It is hard to separate life from work. Everything is interrelated, so this inevitably means eventually talking about the wider aspects of their life. Learning more about them as an individual is key at this stage, so you can plan your sessions to reflect a greater understanding of their preferences and personal style. Possible questions include:

- What else can you tell me about yourself?

- How do you like to learn? Do you learn by doing, reading, talking or thinking?

- How do you like to communicate?

- Are you a 'big picture' or a details person?

Self-awareness and self-evaluation have a huge part to play in coaching, and during this opening Mirror stage we are aiming to help our coachees learn how to evaluate themselves and gain a clearer perception of their own circumstances, personal and/or professional. When someone is feeling dissatisfied or frustrated, it can be helpful to reflect on the positives, as well as what they would like to change, to create a rounded picture of their personal situation.

A key part of good listening means asking follow-up questions to demonstrate that we have heard them, confirm our understanding and to encourage them to share more.

Great follow-ups to this question include:

- What is working and what isn't working? How do you know?

- What is going well and what isn't going so well?'

- What feedback have you had from others?

- What feedback would you give yourself?

- When you look in the mirror, what do you see?

Asking questions is one effective way of exploring our coachee's thoughts, but we can also examine their current situation in a deeper way by making use of exercises or questionnaires. I am a big fan of using a range of coaching tools as this is a great way to add structure and variety to sessions. If your coachee is not particularly forthcoming, is clearly struggling or is quite unfamiliar with the skill of self-analysis, using tools may prove successful in enabling them to understand the questions more easily or approach the process differently; this flexibility and varied approach can help lead each coachee, in whatever way works best, onto a more insightful and relaxed path to self-reflection.

The Magic Wheel

We will be introducing several different coaching tools as we move through the methodology, so here is a great thought-provoking exercise to get us started, The Magic Wheel. With all the activities we will cover, the value is in the discussion which surrounds the exercise, and all the tools I introduce are best used as vehicles to enable you to open up the conversation. I have known this exercise to take up a whole coaching session on its own, so, as with all the models, activities and exercises that follow, don't rush. Take time to create the silence which allows the magic to happen.

EXERCISE: The magic wheel

This exercise works brilliantly within the Mirror stage to help people analyse and compare their current satisfaction levels in different areas of their lives and is designed to stimulate self-reflection and discussion.

Ask your coachee to start by compiling a list of about eight different areas which are important to them in their life or their work. Encourage them to think about which parts of their life they want to focus on. This will depend on the goals and aims of the coaching. The exercise can be completed with a focus on work or home, and can be narrowed down even further to explore specific areas in more detail.

Allow them to take their time to choose these categories. You might start by asking them to write out everything which is important to them and then start to group similar things together, slowly whittling their list down to arrive at about eight items. Typical areas for personal coaching include relationships, health, friends, family, work, finances, house, fitness and work-life balance.

Work can be just one element in the wheel, or alternatively, if the coaching is purely work-focused, the list may include different areas of their role, their responsibilities and their organisational measures of success. They may choose to divide this consideration of their work into sections such as overall career satisfaction, development opportunities, network, relationships with team, manager and/or colleagues. Perhaps instead they want to look at their areas of work accountability, using headings such as planning, budgeting, projects, recruitment, communication etc. The headings are up to them, but the process is the same.

Once they have created a list of about eight areas to focus on, we then ask them to rate each area, giving it a score from one (low) to ten (high) to indicate their overall level of satisfaction.

	Area of focus	Level of satisfaction (0–10)	Comment
1			
2			
3			
4			
5			
6			
7			
8			

With the eight areas identified and scored, we now begin to generate the Magic Wheel. Draw a circle to represent the current situation, and divide the circle into eight wedges, each representing one of the identified areas of focus. Name each wedge with one of the selected areas – the order around the circle is unimportant – and indicate the given score for each area on their wedge, with the centre of the wheel representing a low score, raising through the scores towards ten at the outside. Here is a template to use for this exercise.

Once they have plotted a score for each area, they now join them up to generate an irregular wheel. The question I often ask here is, "How bumpy is your ride?" They are often shocked to see the disparities around the wheel.

My Current Situation

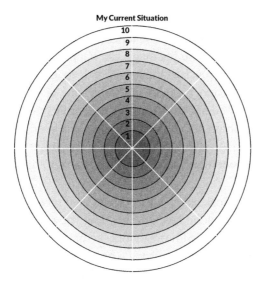

Your role is to ask lots of questions and create a discussion around their score for each area. Ask for examples and clarification and allow them to go back and even change their ratings if they want to. The aim is to enable them to see their present situation more clearly and gain fresh insight. Good questions might include:

- Why have they chosen this area?
- What makes it so important in their life or their role?
- Why have they chosen the rating they have given?

In areas where their ratings are low, you could ask what it would take or what would need to change for the rating to improve. You could ask how long it has been like that, and what they see as the cause and effects; how high the rating would need to go for them to feel satisfied. Would it need to be a ten? Or would eight be good enough?

As coaches, we need to be non-judgemental and objective, and allow time for contemplation to create the silence where the magic can happen. For some coachees, especially those with a deep level of dissatisfaction, it can be quite shocking or upsetting to see this depicted so clearly, especially if they have been putting on a brave face, so be prepared for some emotion. As your discussion continues, it is useful to note down their comments on the table to refer to later.

Here is a real example from someone I recently coached, included with permission. The coachee was struggling with their work-life balance, and long working hours were having a negative effect on family relationships. Here are their chosen areas of focus and their given scores, followed by their comment. This is followed by the completed wheel.

Area of focus	Level of satisfaction (0–10)	Comment
1 Career	9	Love my job.
2 Health and well-being	5	Haven't been to gym or exercised for too long. Need to make more time for this.
3 Finances	7	OK. We earn enough to get by.
4 Friends and social life	6	Lovely friends; don't see them enough.

Area of focus	Level of satisfaction (0–10)	Comment
5 Family relationships	6	This is really important to me. Need to make more time for this as children are growing older and I work long hours. Missed sports day and parents' evening recently due to work commitments.
6 Personal development	9	Good training opportunities at work; feel I am still learning and developing.
7 Work-life balance	4	Am spending too much time at work because I enjoy it, but I can see this is not sustainable.
8 Relationship	6	Central to my life but I can see that my long hours work are causing problems at home.

The bumpy and irregular nature of the wheel provided a sobering visual indicator of their current levels of satisfaction in each of the identified areas, and the discrepancies around the wheel. Seeing this depicted so clearly prompted a valuable discussion and acted as a key motivator for them to make some big life changes.

The Magic Wheel can be an extremely powerful tool. While seeing low ratings can sometimes be quite upsetting, ultimately it can lead towards the positive change they are looking for. Too often I have heard people declare that categories such as family, relationships and work-life balance are of central importance to them, and then seen them give the same categories satisfaction scores under five, as is demonstrated in the example above. Seeing this tension depicted so clearly can lead to revelatory 'light bulb' moments as people start to understand the roots of their dissatisfaction, internal conflict or stress. This type of exercise can also be a really informative way to evaluate the success of the coaching process, as you can repeat the same questions at the end of the programme and compare the answers.

In summary, this deceptively simple initial question – 'What can you tell me about your current situation?' – creates a fantastic opportunity for our coachees to begin to open up, reflect on their life as it is now, and begun to develop their self-awareness. If we can achieve these three things with our first question, then our coaching has got off to a flying start.

4
Question 2 (Mirror)
What would you like
to focus on?

Once our coachee has cleared their head and they have shared the issues which are consuming their energy, they will now be ready to identify some areas to explore through your coaching.

For our coaching to be effective, it is important that each session has a theme or topic to keep it focused. We may veer off the planned theme at times, as other issues present themselves, but it is still our role to steer each coaching session towards a tangible conclusion and set of outcomes. You need your coachee to generate the theme, and to do this you must ask them: 'What would you like to focus on?' There are several alternative ways you could phrase this:

- What would you like to achieve from our coaching?

- How can I help you?

- What are your current priorities?

- What is the best use of our time together?

The fundamental aim of this question is to clarify and agree the areas you will focus on during your coaching. If you are engaging in a one-off coaching session, this question can identify the theme for your meeting; if you are embarking on a longer coaching programme, you may identify several themes, each providing the topic for a specific coaching session. When engaging in personal coaching, the aspirations and goals are set by the individual coachee. If it is business coaching, where the goals are set by the organisation, we may need to provide some steerage to keep the conversation focused on the business targets and KPIs; here the question might take the form of 'Which of your projects or deliverables would you like to focus on?'

It is best if you can contact your coachee before the session to allow them time to think about the topic they would like to address and give you both time to prepare. You need to be flexible about this – there have been many occasions when we have agreed a topic in advance and I have planned accordingly, only to find that on the day the coachee has another more pressing issue to discuss. When this happens, we clearly need to respond to their immediate needs, but we must also bear our wider coaching goals in mind and think about the bigger picture within which we are working, balancing what is urgent and needs addressing now, with what is important for the future.

Your coachee may arrive and present you with a clear agenda, highly focused on what they want to achieve; this is great, but it doesn't always happen. There will be other times when your coachee will just shrug or begin to explain why they didn't complete their 'homework'. It may be that they can't quite verbalise what they want to focus on, or they don't really know what they want – or need – to work on. You may feel the conversation goes round in circles if people lack self-awareness or aren't clear on their goals. When this happens, you need to be prepared to get the coaching back on track and move the discussion forward. Remember that this lack of clarity is often why they have come to you, and so it is your role to create the focus required for success.

Your personal flight path

Here's a model to help which I call the 'personal flight path'. It focuses on your coachee's strengths, areas of expertise and levels of enthusiasm, considering what they feel they are good at and what less so, and on what they do and don't enjoy doing. I use the analogy of travel: what makes them feel they are flying, coasting or exploring and where do they feel they are just parked up while the world passes them by? The richness here, as ever, is in the conversation. We use it at the Mirror stage of the coaching process to help develop the coachee's self-awareness and understand how their levels of expertise and enthusiasm can impact on their achievement of their aspirations and goals. It is particularly helpful when a coachee is feeling stuck – parked up – and doesn't know how to move forward.

When you provide your coachee with the analysis generated by this exercise, you help them create a solid base to look at themselves and their work from new angles, and for identifying opportunities where they could build on their strengths and move forward. They will consider where their expertise and enthusiasm lie, and how they can leverage those to take advantage of the opportunities and minimise some of the roadblocks to progression that may exist in their lives.

Let's now examine each of the four headings from our travel analogy in more detail. They can be considered in terms of a simple matrix, with enthusiasm indicated in the vertical plane, and expertise in the horizontal.

| | EXPERTISE | |
	LOW	HIGH
HIGH	Exploring	Flying
LOW	Parking	Coasting

(ENTHUSIASM indicated on the vertical axis)

Flying

The first heading, 'flying', helps your coachee capture all the things that they really enjoy doing and feel they are good at; here both their enthusiasm and their expertise are high, and they really feel they are flying. We aim to identify their talents, their strengths and the skills which will bring them success, plus their passions and what they really love doing. Encourage them to consider not just current achievements but also the qualities and behaviours that have served them well over time.

Here are some helpful questions to ask:

- Where do your key skills and knowledge lie?

- What do you really enjoy doing?

- What skills come naturally to you?

- What skills, qualifications or experience do you have?

- Which of your achievements are you most proud of?

- What activities give you a sense of energy, satisfaction and confidence?

- Which actions and behaviours sit comfortably with your values, making you proud to call them your strengths?

- What do other people, such as your manager, clients or colleagues, view as your strengths?

Identifying our areas of expertise doesn't always come easily. It can feel uncomfortable to articulate what we feel we are good at, and may people genuinely find it extremely difficult to list their strengths, so if your coachee can't initially describe their areas of expertise, they aren't alone. This might be a good time to gather feedback from colleagues, friends or family members to help support and validate their self-assessment.

Exploring

This section explores areas of potential growth and development opportunities, considering subjects where your coachee's level of enthusiasm is high but their skills base is lower. The personal areas of expertise identified under 'flying' will lead nicely into this discussion about development areas. What skills and knowledge would they really love to explore and enhance?

Good questions to ask here include:

- What would you like to learn to do better?

- Which skills and knowledge areas would you love to develop?

- What opportunities for personal development could you explore?

Coasting

This is an interesting discussion, identifying areas in their life where they have a high level of skill and expertise, but are just 'coasting', well within their comfort zone but without challenge or real enjoyment. Maybe they feel bored, stagnating in certain areas of their job, and they feel a change is necessary to regain their mojo.

I worked with a TV executive who had left his full-time job to become freelance. Even though he had been clear that he wanted to move away from his old areas of expertise, he kept finding himself being pulled back into what he knew and was known to be good at. Now that he had moved out of his organisational role and into freelance employment, it was hugely liberating for him to understand that it was alright to choose where to work – just because he could do it, didn't mean he had to. When he realised this, he gave a huge sigh of relief! He gave himself permission to move on to pastures new, where his passion lay and his skills and experience would fast grow.

Parking

We move finally to discuss the areas where the coachee feels they have neither expertise nor enthusiasm. To continue our travel analogy, this is where our coachee feels 'parked' – areas where they feel they stopped moving forward, their true skills and passions are not being utilised and opportunities are passing them by. They may feel drained, demotivated and bored. If this is a large area, a good starting point could be identifying opportunities to move away from these activities, focusing more time and effort where they have higher levels of expertise and enthusiasm.

I would recommend investing a good amount of time on this personal flight path exercise, particularly if you are embarking on a series of coaching sessions. It can be illuminating, generating insights and ideas and highlighting areas of opportunity where you and your coachee can focus and explore. As you guide your coachee through the generation of their personal flight path, you will thereby define the themes which will shape your coaching work and provide an answer to this second question, 'What would you like us to focus on?'

5
Question 3 (Mirror)
What makes this important to you now?

This third question will conclude our Mirror stage and help us understand the motivation behind the topics your coachee has chosen to cover. The previous question helped clarify *what* they will focus on; this question delves deeper and addresses *why* this is important to them.

What we are essentially asking here is, 'Why this?' and 'Why now?', and this is a good example of two hidden *why* questions within a single *what* question. Fundamentally we want to establish 'Why is this so important to you?', but we are softening it by asking, 'What makes this so important to you now?' We are thinking *why* and asking *what*.

Why this?

Let's explore this 'what' question via its two concealed 'why' elements: 'Why this?' and 'Why now?' To help us examine the first part, here's an example from my own experience.

I remember Sue, a fellow delegate on a training course, many years ago when I first started learning to coach. In a practice exercise, Sue was playing the role of coachee, and she spoke about a holiday with her elderly father, planned for the following year, to visit family in France. She was growing increasingly anxious about her inability to speak French, so her goal was to learn it to at least conversational level before the holiday. She later explained that she had decided on this seemingly straightforward topic because she was a senior manager with a strong sense of personal privacy, and it appeared to be a relatively simple and non-threatening area to discuss in the work environment.

'What motivates you to want to work on this goal?' she was asked; note the 'why' question – 'Why this?' – here rephrased as a 'what' question.

'Well, I've always wanted to learn another language. I feel bad when I visit other countries and so many people can speak English, and French seems the obvious choice.'

'Tell us more,' said the facilitator-coach. This is a great coaching technique to encourage a conversation to develop. Sometimes there is no need to say anything more profound than this deceptively simple invitation to continue.

'Well, we have family in France,' she continued, 'and we don't see them much, and it would be lovely to be able to visit and have proper chats.' She paused, and the coach paused too, holding the silence.

After a few moments, Sue spoke again, this time with some hesitancy. 'My father went to France after the war and met his extended family. He discovered that they had been through an incredibly hard time during the occupation, but he felt frustrated that he couldn't communicate with them properly as neither spoke the other's language. He is frail now and I would like to take him again while he's still able to travel, to chat and share life stories. If I could speak French, then I could translate for my father.' All of a sudden, the tears started; no one was more surprised than she. Once she had regained her composure, she confessed, 'I absolutely didn't see that coming'.

She suddenly realised how personal and profound her true underlying motive behind selecting this topic really was, and also recognised that she had had no idea of the huge emotional significance of her simple ambition to learn French. This multilayered quality can be true of many of our aspirations and goals, and therefore asking these 'why' questions is a powerful way to help our coachees work through the layers to better understand themselves, as well as helping us understand them.

We have looked at the first part of this fascinating question, 'What makes this important to you…?' and we can now turn our attention to the second part of the question, which is to consider the timing: 'Why now?'

Why now?

Here's another example to bring this second hidden element to life. In a recent coaching skills workshop, we were using the MAGIC Methodology questioning arc and one delegate, Muhammed, was talking about his untidy desk. Simple, practical and unsentimental – or so he thought. He explained that he had allowed himself to work in a messy environment for too long and it was hampering his productivity. Within a few minutes he was asked, 'Why do you want to change this now?' He went to answer, and then stopped himself. He hesitated and appeared in deep thought; the magic was happening in the silence.

Suddenly he looked quite startled. 'My father passed away several months ago. My mother and I have been sorting through his things. He was a real hoarder who never seemed to throw anything away, and it's been a really emotional process. If something happens to me, I don't want to leave that amount of mess for other people to sort out.' As he spoke, his speech grew more confident as he began to realise that the process of clearing and sorting through his father's things had been cathartic, and he began to talk of his desire to bring the same structure and simplicity to his working life. He understood that the decluttering had brought order into the mess left by a busy life, and he felt the sense of calm it had created. He paused again and looked as if he had surprised himself. 'I've never thought of it like that before,' he said. This seemingly simple question had enabled him to make connections and understand his motivations in a way that he had never done before.

There is a valuable lesson here. When Sue and Muhammed were asked, 'What makes this important to you now?', both discovered that the goals they had selected for their apparent simplicity and superficial motivations had in fact been masking deeper, more personal drivers. It shows that we can't separate life from work, nor thoughts from feelings; everything overlaps. During coaching, as at any other time, we need to be incredibly sensitive: we may reveal hidden truths and expose forgotten skeletons, and we should be mindful that we can never know others' fragilities or when an underlying emotion will surface. We must tread carefully as they gradually uncover the self within.

When we examine the things which are important to our coachees, we bring into play the question of personal values, the inner beliefs which drive our behaviour; a whole coaching session can usefully be devoted to clarifying these core values. One of the major causes of stress is living a life where our actions conflict with what we value, where our reality does not reflect what is important to us when we look in the mirror. Sometimes our biggest stresses are created by a central misalignment, when our key personal value drivers become out of kilter with our actions, and the ways we spend our days in our personal lives or our jobs. Understanding this often serves as a major catalyst for change.

Let me give some simple examples from my own coaching experience. I had one client who worked in the financial services industry who claimed she truly valued work-life balance and yet frequently found herself working evenings and weekends; another client who said he valued teamwork and collaboration and yet, as a sales executive, found himself in direct competition with colleagues on a daily basis. I've had clients speak of the significance they attach to good health and well-being, while at the same time not eating properly, sleeping well or exercising. Some of these contradictions have already been highlighted through the Magic Wheel exercise we introduced within Question 2, and Question 3 now enables a deeper discussion around these values by enabling our coachees to explore ways to align their values and their actions.

I spoke with a family member recently who was unhappy at work, a fast-paced marketing environment. When we talked about his values, social justice and fairness came out as clear guiding factors for him. His managers had made some decisions with which he disagreed, and he realised that his discomfort was coming from a burning feeling of injustice; 'It's just not fair,' he explained. There was a clear conflict between the culture at work and his deep-seated personal values, and this mismatch was causing him huge stress. He raised his concerns with a colleague, and his response was barely a raised eyebrow: 'That's life, mate. Don't worry about it.' Situations which cause deep discomfort for some people may not even be noticed by others. Identifying personal values, and understanding their alignment with our lives, can be an illuminating exercise and one which can create wonderful insights for our coachees, helping to answer this question of 'Why now?'

Core values

Here is a really simple but effective exercise to help your coachee clarify their true values. I would love you to try this for yourself now, to understand its power.

EXERCISE: Identifying your core values

Here is a list of values:

Achievement	Co-operation	Experience	Individuality
Adventure	Creativity	Expertise	Integrity
Authenticity	Curiosity	Fairness	Intelligence
Authority	Daring	Faith	Love
Autonomy	Decision making	Fame	Loyalty
Balance	Dedication	Family	Making a difference
Beauty	Democracy	Flexibility	Money
Belonging	Directness	Freedom	Optimism
Caring	Discovery	Friendship	Passion
Charity	Diversity	Fun	Quality
Clarity	Duty	Growth	Respect
Collaboration	Empathy	Harmony	Security
Community	Energy	Health	Self-growth
Compassion	Enjoyment	Honesty	Stability
Competition	Environment	Humour	Status
Connection	Ethics	Imagination	Teamwork
Contribution	Excellence	Inclusion	Variety
Control	Excitement	Independence	Wellness

Study this list of values before slowly working your way through the steps that follow. This process can take time and sometimes it is valuable to walk away and come back later, allowing the magic to gently happen in the silence while you busy yourself with something else until greater clarity emerges. Consider the following questions:

1. Start by picking around ten values that feel fundamentally important to you. Do feel free to add to our list.

2. Cut your longlist to the five values that drive you most. You may be able to group similar values together under the same heading within your shortlist. Don't rush.

3. Now, rank those top five values in order of their importance to you. To help you determine levels of importance, consider whether you would be happy and excited, or disappointed and upset, if the significance of each value within your life were to change. Bear in mind that values that were important to you in the past may not be so relevant now. For example, the importance of career progression may be superseded by work-life balance if your family circumstances change.

4. For each of the five values on your shortlist, the next step is to assess how and where you feel each value is currently being expressed, and then rate your level of satisfaction with this answer. You may choose to consider this in relation to your life and work separately, or you may choose to view your life as a whole.

5. It might help to think of this in a particular context. For example, if you are focusing on your professional life and have chosen 'autonomy' as a key value, ask yourself how much you feel that you are able to demonstrate autonomy at work. Do you feel opportunities for autonomous working are

almost totally absent, or is it something you feel is prioritised? Then consider how satisfied you are with your answer to the previous question, using a scale of one to five where one represents dissatisfied and five represents greatly satisfied.

	My top values	Current expression in my life	Satisfaction level 1 (low)–5 (high)
1			
2			
3			
4			
5			

As you look at your results, you may find that your satisfaction levels are mostly high, with the top values being strongly expressed within your life. When this happens, life will feel pretty good. However, you may find the opposite is the case, with disappointingly low scores across the board.

Another possibility is that your key values may be little expressed within your life, while those you rank lower receive greater expression. Low scores and mismatches will leave you feeling demotivated and frustrated, with a sense that things just aren't right. Even if your scores are high, you may still feel dissatisfied or unfulfilled. If this is the case, I ask you to think again about what is genuinely important to you. Are you being honest and true to yourself? Make sure you aren't prioritising the values you think you should hold, or of those around you. This is about you, no one else. As part of this exercise, it can be helpful to spend time defining what each value means to you, because words can mean such different things to different people. It can also be illuminating to analyse why the chosen values feel so important.

With your top five values in mind, particularly those you scored with the lowest satisfaction levels, and an awareness of your longlist of ten, ask yourself what actions you could take to enable more of your values to be expressed more frequently? In many cases, even small changes to how you work and live can reap huge benefits for you.

Let us continue with the example of 'autonomy' at work to illustrate this. If you had rated your satisfaction level to be two out of five, suggesting you have a low satisfaction level with the degree of autonomy you have at work, you could explore what actions you could take to improve the situation. One option might be to volunteer to own a project or lead a piece of work; this would provide the freedom to make decisions and take responsibility, and a chance to exercise a high degree of control. Perhaps ask colleagues at work if they can help with identifying opportunities? In some cases, if very few – or possibly even none – of your core values are being adequately expressed, you may need to consider a more impactful change. In a work context, this may even mean motivating yourself to start looking for a role more closely aligned with your core values.

As we journey through life, our values may change over time. Fun, socialising and excitement may be replaced by career progression and promotion, which in turn may be replaced by work-life balance and security. It is important to keep in touch with your guiding principles, and therefore it is worth revisiting this exercise regularly, particularly when you sense that things feel wrong, to ensure that the choices you make as you go through your life and your career line up with your core values at that time. There is plenty of research to suggest that higher levels of satisfaction at work are achieved when there is a strong alignment between personal values and the organisational or work-based values.

In her article 'The Top 5 Tips for Understanding your Values' shared by the Association for Coaching, Suzanne Henwood writes, 'your values are the keys to your motivation – if you want to live life to the full and know you are fulfilling your unique purpose in life, find out what your values are and live to meet them fully at every opportunity.'

If your coachee struggles to identify or articulate their values, here are some discussion points which could help:

- **Peak moments:** Ask them to think about times when they have been really energised and motivated or fulfilled and satisfied. What was happening then? Where were they? What were they doing at the time? What were their personal circumstances? Who were they with? Which values were being expressed at this time, and how?

- **Low moments:** Ask them to consider occasions when they were angry, upset, demotivated, frustrated or stressed. What were they doing at the time? Who were they with? What were their personal circumstances? Did they feel that something was missing or should have been done differently? Was this because one of their key values was absent, being suppressed or being challenged? We might not recognise our values until something, or someone, means they are not being honoured.

- **Must haves:** Ask them what they feel they 'must have' in their life to be fulfilled? It might be love, freedom, independence or perhaps security. Ask them to think about what these concepts really mean to them as individuals?

- **Critical moments:** Ask them to recall a time when they have had to make a decision that they found particularly difficult. What was it that finally persuaded them to go in one direction or another? Can they link this choice with a core value?

This is an exercise to enable your coachee to learn more about their key personal drivers and it is important to emphasise that there are no right or wrong values; they are deeply personal, and closely reflect our experiences, our culture and even our personalities. This is a key moment for you as a coach to really practice being non-judgemental.

One of the pivotal moments in my adult life came about fifteen years ago when I was at the airport ready to fly to Europe for a few days to run a training course. I was a single mum with three children under ten, and the preparation for this work trip had caused me an extraordinary amount of stress. As I hurried through the queues, I was worrying about homework, lunch boxes and World Book Day costumes (every parent of school-age children will feel my angst there!). I clearly recall stopping suddenly on the concourse at

Heathrow and weeping, overwhelmed by the pressure. I asked myself, 'Why am I doing this overseas work trip? Is it really worth it? Does my family need me more?'

At that moment, I made a decision: I would not do it again. It clashed too much with my belief in the importance of family values, particularly because of my personal circumstances, and fighting this was making me miserable. I didn't go on another overnight work trip for over ten years. I totally understand that many of my trainer colleagues really enjoy regular trips away. It works fine for them and their circumstances, but for me at that time, they were awful. Making a clear decision to refuse any work that took me away from home overnight from then on gave me a huge sense of clarity about my values and an overwhelming sense of relief. Every time I was subsequently offered a work trip, I didn't agonise about whether or not I should accept, I just said 'no'. I gave the overnight work to colleagues who enjoyed it and thanked me for it, and I felt I was able to live in closer alignment with my personal values, and I was more present for my children while being able to earn a living too. Win-win-win.

This brings us to the end of the Mirror section of the MAGIC Methodology. This section has demonstrated that using this framework offers three key benefits:

- A valuable opportunity to understand our coachee's current situation.

- An identification of the topics they would like to address.

- The chance to explore why these topics are currently so important to your coachee.

The first three questions, and the exercises provided, have all asked us to consider the areas of self-awareness, self-evaluation and self-assessment and we have seen how this requires sensitive enquiry, warmth, honesty and a non-judgemental approach. After the discussions provoked by these questions, which I am sure will have been insightful and stimulating, you will be well equipped to move on to the next section, where you ask your coachee to start to explore their hopes, dreams, vision and aspirations, before identifying specific goals to work towards.

6

Question 4 (Aspirations)

If you had a magic wand, what would you like to achieve?

This coaching question is the absolute favourite of many coaches! Let us consider why.

In our daily lives, we are often particularly good at thinking of things we can't do and reasons why things won't work. We make plans and arrangements based on what we feel to be possible, simple, affordable and achievable, within all the constraints imposed by the real world. When we ask our coachees to share their goals with us, they often don't know where to start. They may find it easy to talk about tasks they would like to complete and small changes they would like to make but can often be more reticent when it comes to sharing their wider hopes and aspirations for fear of seeming unrealistic. The power of this wonderful question is that the magic wand gives permission to temporarily step outside these everyday constraints that hamper so much of our creativity, and instead imagine what we would do if absolutely anything were possible.

You might be familiar with the adage, 'If you always do what you've always done, you always get what you've always gotten.' This idea is reflected in the saying often attributed, apparently mistakenly, to Einstein, that insanity is repeating the same thing again and again and expecting a different result. We want our coaching to facilitate a process of our coachee's questioning their thinking; only then can they start to act differently, and change will then follow.

To encourage and enable our coachees to challenge and change their thinking, it can be very effective to start with a broad overview, widely considering the bigger picture, imagining possibilities and asking 'What if…?' questions, before we then start focusing more narrowly to identify clear goals and tangible targets. If we rush into the details and start asking our coachees to articulate a clear goal too early in the process, in my experience, people often become stuck and don't know where to start. I therefore recommend that we start this section of the coaching by asking a wide-open question, to get the conversation started and fire up our coachee's imagination: 'If you had a magic wand, what would you like to achieve?'

This is a moment where we really have to allow our coachee time to think and reflect. It can be a hard question to answer. We need to be supportive, compassionate and non-judgemental; be aware that as well as just identifying possible answers, your coachee may also be deciding whether they feel able to share hopes and dreams that they may have never voiced before. The discussion prompted by this question can encompass so much more than a goal or a target; it can explore your coachee's whole *raison d'être,* their deeper purpose in life, their *Why.*

This question can be worded in many ways, all with the same intention. Some possible examples include:

- What would you aim for if you knew you couldn't fail?

- What would you do if all constraints were removed?

- What is your ideal outcome?

If we haven't yet established a firm foundation of trust and created an atmosphere of openness and honesty, we won't get far with this question. Our body language, the expression on our face and our response as the coachee begins to open up will be fundamental influencers when they are deciding how honest they can afford to be in their answer to you today. You may find you hear some pretty crazy dreams at this stage. When I ask this question, people often say things like,

'You will probably think this is wild, but I have always wanted to...', or 'Don't laugh, but I would really love to...'. Don't worry: later in the process we will be working with our coachees to turn their aspirations into more practical goals, so don't be afraid to allow them to dream big for a while. It may at least serve to stimulate their creativity, and this will, in turn, help engage and motivate them.

When we delve into the realm of aspirations and goals, and our coachees start to share their inner thoughts about what they would really like to achieve, our aim is to help them become absorbed in this vision of their future selves (their Future Me): hearing it, feeling it, touching it, seeing it, smelling it, soaking up the wonderful excitement of actually being there one day. This creates the kind of motivation that enables us to keep going through tougher times and binds the coachee to the process of building this future. Sometimes this process can lead them to realise that they are aiming for a target which is not actually their real goal; it could be an artefact, a relic from a previous age, a distraction or even a goal imposed on them by somebody else.

Sometimes we hanker after a particular destination, only to realise when we arrive that we didn't want to go there after all. As an example, a colleague of mine recently coached a senior manager who had been determined to win a promotion, only to find that, when she achieved her dream position, she became miserable and quickly realised that she had actually been in her perfect job all along; an unfortunate outcome. It is our job to make sure that our coachee has chosen an aspiration and a goal which really comes from within, and is not just what they used to want, what they think they want, what they feel they ought to want, or what other people want for them.

Finding harmony

A fantastic model to help people think through their aspirations and dreams is to consider the Japanese concept of 'ikigai'. The word has no direct English translation, but can be understood variously as your purpose, your motivation and the reason you get up in the morning. In Japan it is seen as a multifaceted and nuanced concept which can be used to describe someone's dreams and that which drives them. It is the process of capturing the happiness in living, and a concept that can be applied beautifully to our work as coaches.

Although ikigai has long been important in Japanese culture, it only became widely known after the publication in 1966 of *Ikigai-ni-Tsuite*, the seminal work by the Japanese psychiatrist Mieko Kamiya. Inspired by her patients and the sense of meaninglessness many of them described, she became fascinated by 'What makes life worth living' or 'On the meaning of life', as the title can be roughly understood, although it is not yet translated or published in English (see Kemp). As Yukari Mitsuhashi describes, Kamiya 'explains that as a word, ikigai is similar to "happiness" but has a subtle difference', for 'Ikigai is what allows you to look forward to the future even if you're miserable right now.' I think this is a wonderful quote, helping us to keep going through tough times. Even if things feel difficult or wrong now, when you have a strong goal that you're working towards, then you can be said to have found your ikigai.

Here I share my own simplified version of this concept, which I call Finding Harmony. This visual representation and the process of filling it in is a useful coaching exercise, and there is great value in a discussion to determine the characteristics of the factors, beliefs and influences that motivate us most strongly at any one time.

EXERCISE: Finding my harmony

To create harmony and balance in our lives, we shall consider four key elements:

- What I love
- What I am good at
- How I can help the world
- How I can earn a living

If we can create a life for ourselves that combines what we love with what we are good at, we can help the world and earn a living too, then this is where harmony and balance can be said to lie.

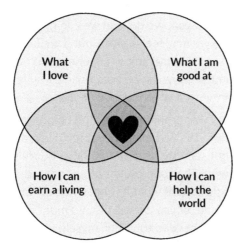

However, we don't need to find all four elements from the same areas of our life. We may find that our jobs or careers fulfil some part of the equation, while our hobbies, families or other parts of our lives complete the remaining elements.

Consider the following examples:

- If we earn a living from something we are good at or feel we are doing good in the world, but we don't love what we do, we may be comfortable at work and financially but still have a feeling of emptiness.

- I have a friend who is an accountant. She takes a pragmatic approach to her job: 'I am good at it, I offer a good service, it pays the bills and I will always have work, but I could never say I love what I do.' While her work alone may not offer complete fulfilment, I still think she has created harmony and balance. Her real passion is horses, and it is her accountancy work that funds this hobby, so in her life as a whole, she has found her harmony.

- If we love what we do, and we can get paid to do it, then we may feel excited, but if we lack the relevant skills, training or experience to do it well, this enthusiasm can be accompanied by feelings of uncertainty, low confidence or stress.

- When I was promoted to my first managerial position, this was much how I felt. I loved my new job, but secretly worried that I was out of my depth and would be soon caught out as a fraud. I had a classic case of what has been named 'imposter syndrome', which we will discuss more in the next chapter. I needed to upskill myself, and fast.

- If we love what we do and are good at it, plus we can earn a living doing it, but we feel it doesn't serve the world well in some way, then we may feel satisfied but not useful. An acquaintance with a high-flying corporate job recently confessed that she had always loved her job but had a nagging feeling that she now wanted to give something back to society, having become a little disillusioned as she got older. My daughter was taught by a teacher who had recently embarked on a total career change, leaving the world of finance for the classroom because he wanted to seek a new form of personal fulfilment. The Covid-19 pandemic, which changed the world so drastically, seems to have crystalised for many people this sense of needing a greater purpose and also provided an opportunity for change.

- If we love what we do, are good at it but we can't get paid for it, then we may gain fulfilment, but we will need to find another route to financial stability.

- I have a friend who works for a small charity. She loves what she does, there is an enormous need for the wonderful service they provide, but as she wryly comments, she certainly isn't in it for the money, describing herself as happy and fulfilled, but poor!

Our goal, therefore, is to help our coachee to create a life where they can hold all four elements in harmony. Someone with a fulfilling job that they excel at, and which provides financial security, plus a hobby, family or volunteering role that they love, may well have found true harmony. To use this as a coaching exercise, I suggest you share this model and talk through each area, asking questions to promote discussion and reflection and help your coachee consider how they might create greater harmony in their life.

Not so long ago, I turned fifty. Like many others reaching this significant milestone, I spent a considerable amount of time in the months leading up to it thinking about how I would like to spend the next ten years of my working life. I have been hugely fortunate. I love my work as a trainer and a coach – it is stimulating, varied, challenging, rewarding and flexible. It has enabled me to build a successful career as a working mum while rarely having to miss a school sports day, concert or class assembly. I was able to build it this way, and I made choices along the way to honour my personal values and my commitment to those I loved, and what I loved.

Sometimes the 'magic wand' question will lead coachees to articulate a hidden desire, something they have held in their head as an aspiration for years, often without ever examining it. The Aspirations stage of the MAGIC Methodology enables them to examine such ambitions and decide whether they really want what they think they want. It is so important to get this right because the most well-defined goals and plans will lead a person down the wrong path if the presumed aspiration to which they are leading just isn't correct.

It is therefore important to spend time at this stage, helping coachees work through their thoughts and hear them reflected by us, even if they appear to have their aspirations and goals already clearly defined. When they give voice to their hidden dreams and start exploring them in detail, sometimes we find that they pivot in their thinking, recognising that this dream and their whole aspiration may need to change significantly. I have encountered this numerous times, and here is a great example of such a shift from a recent delegate on a coaching course, Nigel.

I was coaching a small group from the airline industry, and as we progressed through the coaching arc, I asked Nigel our fourth question: 'If you had a magic wand, what would you like to achieve?'

'I want to give up shift work. I've had enough of getting up at 4am and working weekends and bank holidays. I want to be there for my children at weekends,' he replied. He talked about wanting to work regular nine-to-five hours rather than his current variable shift pattern, and spoke about the benefits he associated with working regular hours: 'I'll have weekends off work. I'll be home in the evenings. It sounds great.'

He was then asked why he had done shift work for so long and why he hadn't made this change already. He began to articulate the benefits of shift work – he liked the flexibility, 'I like driving to work and avoiding the traffic' – but then he paused for a few minutes. He went on, 'I see my children at the beginning or end of every day. I can swap shifts and sometimes get almost a week off without using any annual leave. I often do that at half term.' He paused again. We waited, and I could almost see the cogs in his brain whirring away.

'Actually,' he said slowly, 'shift work is brilliant. Working nine-to-five would mean I would get stuck in the rush hour traffic twice a day. I would never see my children properly during the week because I'd be gone before they get up and not home until bedtime. I could only go shopping at the weekends when it is busy as everyone else is off too. I'd have to work every day of half term. I've been moaning about shift work for years and dreaming about how I wanted to change my life, but actually that's not what I want at all. What I have right here and now actually works brilliantly for me and my family, I just didn't see it.'

During the course of this short conversation, his entire focus had changed. He began to talk about appreciating the benefits of his work more, and of seeking new challenges, development opportunities and getting more involved in interesting projects within his current role. As the coach, I had not really said much at all, but what I had done was ask questions to help him focus his thoughts, articulate his thoughts and examine them. As he had worked through the Aspirations stage of the coaching, what had changed was his mindset, and he had done it for himself. He looked slightly shell-shocked but happy. The magic had happened in the silence.

What does success mean for you?

You might think that the meaning of 'success' is straightforward enough. The word can, after all, be found in every dictionary and you might therefore be tempted to think that it has a meaning that's common to everyone, but let's examine this in a little more detail.

The *Cambridge Dictionary* definition of 'success' is 'the achieving of the results wanted or hoped for; something that achieves positive results'; while Collins' is 'the achievement of something that you have been trying to do.' So far, so good. Few would argue with these. This second dictionary offered an additional definition: 'Success is the achievement of a high position in a particular field, for example in business or politics.' More people would take issue with defining success by public status, as is implied here, I think. A further definition from the same dictionary is equally debateable: 'Someone or something that is a success, achieves a high position, makes a lot of money, or is admired a great deal.' That isn't my definition of success, and it may not be yours either. The truth is that success means a range of things to different people. The older, and possibly wiser (!), that I become, the more I realise how differently we all define, and thus value, success.

The personal vision statement

A great exercise at this point would be for your coachee to create a 'personal vision statement', which encapsulates their aspirations and defines what success looks like for them. This is a big-picture statement and is best articulated in the present tense. You may wish to try creating your own as an exercise now. Here's an extract from mine and a bit of the background to it.

A year or two ago, I asked myself the question, 'If you had a magic wand, what would you like to achieve?' – or rather my husband, who is an excellent coach himself, asked me this question as part of a conversation about plans for our next decade.

'I'd like to write a book about coaching,' I replied. 'I have so many thoughts in my head I would like to share, so much that I have learned through coaching and training coaches and leaders over the last twenty years, that I have always wanted to get it all in one place, clearly laid out and explained.'

Hearing myself outlining my goals, I captured this thought and created an aspirational vision of my future:

> 'I am a published author. I have completed a book about the magical power of coaching and devised a series of workshops to run alongside it, offering readers the opportunity to translate the knowledge they gain into practical skills. We have a methodology outlined in a book, an e-book and an audiobook. We have an online course, with different versions for workplace manager-coaches and for independent personal coaches, a workbook and an accompanying certificate to celebrate the professional development of our delegates. We also have a beautiful website, with a community of alumni supporting each other in their coaching journey.'

That's how my vision of the future looked and felt a few years ago, and you are reading the results of these dreams right now!

Creating a personal vision statement can be a little like creating a mood board for a decorating project. Coachees who particularly learn visually may use images and diagrams, others will prefer words and phrases, and creative coachees may use texture and colour. However you and your coachee chose to create this vision, it will be a great way to capture the incredible outpourings that can result from this inspiring and liberating question, 'If you had a magic wand, what would you like to achieve?'

7
Question 5 (Aspirations)
How would you describe the bridge you will need to cross to achieve this aspiration?

After generating a vision of the future with your coachee via the previous question, this one seeks to begin clarifying the nature of the gap between the aspirations they have defined and their current reality. It is a great question to help you delve deeper together, and one with great potential and power, so we must allow time for self-reflection and assessment. Their degree of self-awareness will have a big impact on how successfully they can both conceive and accurately describe this bridge. If they don't truly know where they are starting from, it is difficult for them to judge the nature of the gap between their present reality and their future aspirations.

When we ask this question, be prepared for a wide range of answers. Sometimes they might use highly visual terms as though the bridge were right before them. They will describe its size: 'It's huge' or 'It isn't actually that big;' its appearance: 'It's a rickety, swinging footbridge,' 'It's a series of rocks in a small stream;' or the anticipated challenges of crossing it: 'I have to leap from rock to rock across fast-flowing water,' 'It feels unsafe beneath my feet.' Sometimes they may describe the feeling the bridge invokes, whether it feels 'terrifying' or 'overwhelming', 'energising' or 'exciting'. Most inspiringly of all, it is sometimes envisioned as 'a bridge to a new world'.

The language used to describe the bridge is incredibly useful in helping you know how best to guide the coachee so that they come to understand that, however they conceive the bridge, the point is that it is there. There is a bridge that will allow them to cross from one place (the current situation) to the other (their imagined future), and it isn't an obstacle, like an insurmountable wall or a mountain, but a structure designed to aid passage, and we will help them plan and traverse their way across.

Feedback

Some coachees will balk when asked to describe an imaginary bridge. If we have already helped our coachee through the process of learning how to assess their current situation accurately and honestly, answering this question will feel a little easier. If they still find it hard to establish their starting point and appear lost when considering the journey ahead, this might be a good time for the coachee to seek out further information via feedback.

Feedback comes in many forms. If you are coaching them as their manager, you may be well placed here to offer feedback yourself, based on your observations and knowledge of their performance at work. If you are an external or independent coach, this can be more difficult. You may not know your coachee well, if at all, and you will probably not have enough evidence or examples to enable you to offer your coachee an opinion or any credible feedback; it may actually be inappropriate in your role as their coach for you to offer your thoughts. An alternative that may work well would be for them to collect feedback from colleagues, friends or others who know them well. Some people 'big themselves up', others put themselves down, and some have received so little feedback that they have no idea how they are perceived by others.

I often find it useful, to assist my coachee in the developing their self-awareness, to start my coaching by asking them to gather feedback from colleagues, clients or stakeholders, perhaps by arranging a few coffee meetings, or even by sending out a short questionnaire to gather a range of views to feed into the process. Sending out the same form at the end of a

coaching process can also be an excellent way of mea-
suring progress and therefore assessing the impact
and success of the coaching.

I remember a career-coaching session with Dan, an
experienced manager approaching his mid-forties
who had recently been made redundant and was
assessing where to go next. He aspired to move
into a managerial position within the high-pressure
world of software sales, but when I asked him about
the bridge he would need to cross to achieve this, he
found he couldn't answer it. He explained, 'I can't
judge the size of the gap because I have absolutely no
idea what my strengths are. I appear to have had a
reasonably successful career so far across a period of
over twenty years, but I have never had a single helpful performance appraisal, and no one has ever given
me any feedback.' He struggled to describe the bridge
because he felt unable to assess his starting point with
any degree of certainty or accuracy.

I encouraged Dan to go out and seek some feedback
from others to help him in the process going forward,
but I also wondered about his observation that he had
never received feedback. I didn't doubt that he had
never had a helpful appraisal, nor that he had never
been sat down for a formal discussion of his strengths
and development areas. In my experience, however,
feedback is all around us if we look for it. It is evident
in people's responses to us, in their enthusiasm or lack
of it for our ideas and our contributions; it is there in

the expression on their faces and in the actions they take; it is present in the results that we do, or don't, achieve. Although he had never been given effective feedback directly, it also seemed that perhaps he had not been aware of the feedback which constantly surrounded and influenced him. Whatever the reason, it remained the case that Dan had never established a clear outline of his strengths and development areas, and this was holding him back.

In these situations, where people desperately need or are actively craving feedback, the advice we can give them is simple. Here's what I would say to someone in that situation:

- **Look out for it:** Feedback about your performance is all around you if you open your eyes and ears to it.

- **Ask for it:** Make a point of asking people what they think of your contribution and your ideas. If you deliver a presentation or chair a meeting, casually asking people 'How do you think that went?' is a great tactic, and the replies may reveal an area of weakness or a performance gap, or boost your confidence with some complimentary observations.

- **Listen well when you do receive it:** When receiving feedback, it is all too easy to become defensive and not properly listen. We may respond with dismissive or deflective comments – 'I only said that because I was rushing,' 'I don't normally behave that way,' 'It was only because I was stressed' – instead of making a conscious effort to listen to what people are trying to tell us. There will be time when feedback is hard to hear, or when it isn't delivered skilfully or tactfully, but there may still be significant value in what is being said, so my advice is always to stop and listen. Ask questions to make sure you understand what you are being told: 'Can you give me an example of when I did that?', 'Can you be more specific?' or 'Have you seen me do that on other occasions?' These are all great questions which can help you maximise the power of the feedback you are being given.

- **Thank people for it:** Demonstrating your gratitude, 'Thanks for being so honest' or 'Thank you for sharing your thoughts with me,' is an appropriate response to feedback, whether it has been motivational or developmental. It is good to show that we appreciate the time people have taken to generate and then deliver the feedback, and sometimes the bravery they have shown in being honest, however hard it might have been for both them and you. You may even receive a wonderful compliment – they may love working with you – and the feedback you get may make your day!

- **Act on it:** Actually doing something about the feedback that you receive can often be the hardest part of the process. It can be uncomfortable to hear home truths and it takes courage to admit that we aren't always right, but now is an opportunity to make the necessary changes, however difficult that might be.

Let's return to Dan. Based on this conversation, I set him the task of going out and gathering clear, evidence-based feedback from people who had worked with him and knew him well, and the results were a revelation to him. He finally felt that he had an accurate understanding of how he was perceived by others and an objective assessment of his skills and weaker areas. Now he was able to describe the bridge: it was 'big and scary but definitely an achievable challenge, not an insurmountable obstacle,' and so our journey could begin.

We have so far learned to explore and assess our current situation and how to identify our desired destination. We know we have a distance to travel, but an accurate understanding of the starting point is a key part of helping our coachees to describe the bridge that lies ahead. Our next question, the final question in the Aspirations stage, is where we examine what has stopped us proceeding before now.

8
Question 6 (Aspirations)
What has stopped you crossing this bridge before now?

This is a huge question, and one that needs to be approached with great sensitivity and empathy.

We know that we are all busy, juggling many different areas of responsibility in our lives, and we can be easily distracted from working on our goals in favour of more pressing deadlines. However, when someone has a realistic and well-defined aspiration, and they appear to have the necessary enthusiasm and expertise, but they haven't yet crossed the bridge, there must clearly be a blockage somewhere. When I ask coachees what has stopped them from crossing before now, finding the time is often cited as the biggest barrier. They described how they haven't had the time available to devote to the process of achieving their aspirations, and other things have got in the way. In my experience, this is an excuse that is often masking a deeper motive, because we usually create time for the things we genuinely want to do.

Question 6: 'What has stopped you crossing the bridge before now?' is asked at this stage because if we hope to generate a different outcome on this occasion, we need to uncover and examine these obstacles that have so far blocked our path. Only if we have identified the obstructions can we begin to generate the ideas, plans and even alternative routes that will enable us to finally cross the bridge where previous attempts have failed.

As coaches, we can sometimes feel like detectives, trying to decipher what is really going on beneath the surface. My family are great Sherlock Holmes fans, and in *A Scandal in Bohemia*, Holmes reproaches Watson, 'You see, but you do not observe.' We too should heed these words, for as coaches, we need to see *and* observe. As well as listening to what is being said, we need also to be aware of what is not being said, of how things are being said, of what is being revealed by our coachee's body language and in their eyes, by their tone of voice and the expression on their face. Like Holmes, we must see, observe and also deduce.

When people blame a lack of time in response to this question, we need to pause and wait. Create some silence, and we may find that their first answer is followed by a second response, usually deeper, more personal and even emotional. One example of this is fear, and all too often this is fear of failure.

Fear of failure

Here is an example of this, from a recent coaching session that I ran within an educational organisation. Two experienced senior managers, Aidan and Brian, were taking turns to coach each other within the group setting. Both were intelligent, well-educated, open-minded and successful men with a good level of self-awareness, and yet, as I watched, both came to understand that a fear of failure was holding them back.

Aidan went first and explained that his goal was to start cycling to work. He had already planned his route and researched suitable road bikes. Brian followed our questioning arc and, within ten minutes, Aidan was being asked what was stopping him from cycling to work now. 'I haven't had time to buy the gear,' he said. Then he paused and we waited.

'That's not the true reason,' he added, hesitatingly. 'There's something else… What if I fail? What if I turn up to the office clad in full Lycra, and everyone thinks it is fascinating and takes an interest… and then it proves too much for me… and I stop? Everyone will know I've failed! So, it's easier not to start.' This was a searingly honest response and a revelation to us all, including Aidan himself.

The two men then swapped over. Brian explained that his goal was to learn to speak Italian. His wife was from Italy, and he wanted to be able to speak with her family and join in their family discussions; more profoundly, he wanted to demonstrate his love and respect for her by learning her home language. He explained to Aidan that he had been wanting to do it for ages. He was keen and motivated, but he hadn't managed to get around to it because he was always so busy. 'It's lack of time that's been stopping me,' he said, before stopping for a moment or two.

'To be honest, I probably do have the time. I have a long commute and learning Italian would be a productive use of this time. I don't know why I haven't done it yet.' Aidan did well to hold the silence, and we waited. Brian seemed lost in thought, before eventually he continued. 'Actually, I do know why I haven't done it. However much hard work I put in, and however good I become, I will never be as good as her. She will always be correcting me and she speaks excellent English, so we can already communicate perfectly well. I will never match her easy familiarity with the language and so I know that I will never be satisfied. I will always think I have failed, so it is easier not to try.' He paused, looking a bit stunned – he had finally worked out what was really stopping him.

This was just a one-day training course, and I haven't seen either of the men again. I always wonder if they managed to move forward and achieve their goals; I really hope they did.

Fear of failure is a significant blocker experienced by many adults, but other fears can stop us too.

Fear of change

Here is another simple and moving example showing how *fear of change* can also impede progression.

A coaching programme attendee shared her goal of clearing out her children's playroom and turning it into a home office. 'I don't know why I don't just do it,' she said. 'There's nothing I love more than a good old clear-out, and I am forever emptying cupboards and sorting clutter at home.'

She was gently asked, 'What's stopping you this time?'

'I *am* busy, but shortage of time is just an excuse.' She paused for a moment as the group silently waited, and then her eyes welled up. 'I know what it is,' she said slowly. 'I'm not ready for my children's childhood to be over. I don't want them to grow out of needing a playroom.' I can relate to this so strongly that my eyes are welling up as I write this. 'Oh,' she said, 'I think

I am going to cry!' She took time to gather herself, before taking a few deep breaths. 'Wow,' she said at last.

The following day, I received a photo of her clearing out the room. 'I have done it!' she declared. 'As soon as I realised what was stopping me, it lost its power. I took a few photos of the room to keep as a memory and then I accepted that it is time for us all to move forward.' Recognising what was stopping her and articulating what was happening had been power-fully liberating. As she said, she had 'named it and tamed it'.

Fear of being found out

Fear of being 'found out' is often referred to as 'impos-ter syndrome'. In an article for the International Coaching Federation in 2018, Kim Morgan explains 'If you experience imposter syndrome, you may fear that you are going to be "found out", discount your successes by putting them down to luck, think anyone could do what you do, negate your accomplishments, feel like you don't have the right to be doing what you are doing or have a sense that you don't belong where you are'.

Imposter syndrome often develops or increases in times of change, for example when we are going through a career transition, seeking a promotion or working to achieve a big, slightly scary goal. If you hear your coachee putting themselves down or comparing themselves negatively to others, they may be suffering from imposter syndrome. Clues can include:

- Self-criticism: 'I am so stupid,' 'Why do I always get things wrong?'

- Excessive self-reliance: 'I can't ask for help or people will think I am incompetent.'

- Underestimating or negating their own abilities: 'Other people's ideas always seem to be better than mine.'

- A lack of confidence in their own abilities or the value of their opinions: 'I don't know enough.'

- Procrastination, not starting things in case they fail: 'I'll do it later when I am more prepared.'

- Perfectionism, having unrealistically high expectations of themselves: 'I can't make even the smallest mistake because everyone will think I am incapable.'

- Imposing unrealistic expectations on themselves: 'I should be able to do everything successfully.'

If you suspect that your coachee is demonstrating signs of imposter syndrome, they are not alone. According to Rubinstein, studies suggest that more than 70% of people will experience imposter syndrome at some point in their lives. You can help your coachee by guiding them in the process of challenging their doubts about their competence, their poor likelihood of success, or beliefs that their voice does not deserve to be heard.

Ask if they have any evidence to support these fears, or examples and illustrations of the worst-case scenarios which they describe. 'What is the worst that can happen?' is a great question to use, followed by 'How likely is that to happen?' and 'If it did happen, how bad would it really be?' Encourage them to talk more about their past successes and achievements. Help them consider things more proportionately and think more positively if they are catastrophising or exaggerating the likelihood of disaster if they move ahead in pursuit of their aspirations and goals. Don't let them talk themselves into believing that they don't deserve success, whatever that means to them. They deserve success just as much as anyone else, and as coaches we can play a wonderful part in helping them articulate, work towards and ultimately achieve their aspirations.

The issues we discuss while answering this question may well appear again later in our coaching, as barriers, obstacles or long-held fears can often re-emerge as we move forward. The time invested at this stage can therefore really help develop a good level of self-awareness which can help us throughout the coaching process.

QUESTION 6 (ASPIRATIONS)

We have now completed our exploration of the second stage of the MAGIC Methodology, Aspirations. We have waved a magic wand and revealed what our coachee would really love to achieve, they have described the bridge they will need to cross to achieve this aspiration, and we have discussed the factors which have prevented achieving them already. After this rich and meaningful conversation, we are ready to move on to focus on turning these Aspirations into tangible and achievable Goals.

9

Question 7 (Goals)

Can you create a clear goal, achievable within a realistic timeframe?

Over 100 years ago, the hugely successful Scottish-born American industrialist and philanthropist Andrew Carnegie stated that 'If you want to be happy, set a goal that commands your thoughts, liberates your energy and inspires your hopes.' This is still excellent advice today.

A centrally important element of coaching is the setting of goals – 'I want to achieve X outcome by Y date' – and this is one of the key aspects that differentiates a coaching conversation from a supportive chat. I have always been taught that, at the start of a coaching relationship, it is key to agree clear, measurable and motivational goals so that everyone is clear on the aims and scope of the coaching, what will be achieved and why the coaching has been organised.

Many coaching models open with this stage, asking questions like, 'What are your goals? What specifically do you want to achieve?' In my experience this is rarely successful: many people don't know what they want to achieve and are unable to articulate a clearly defined and specific goal, they just know that something feels wrong or they want to achieve more. They know things might need to change, and they might know they can't do it alone, but perhaps they don't know what success in achieving this looks like for them, and that is why they have turned to coaching to help.

This is why our MAGIC Methodology does not begin with goal-setting questions at the outset of the coaching. We begin with a discussion about the coachee's current situation. I find that people often want you first to understand their current reality because their goals only make sense against this background. Only then, once we have established a foundation of trust, provided an opportunity for them to outline their current circumstances and their future aspirations, listened and empathised, do I feel our coachees are ready to move on. We can begin to dream big ambitious dreams, creating a vision of the future, but only after we have done the exploratory work which has led us to the stage we are at now. With the big picture in place, now is the time to narrow the focus and guide our coachee through the process of identifying to create a clear and tangible goal statement which encapsulates exactly what they want to achieve.

Goal setting is an essential part of effective coaching because it gives us a destination to aim towards, creating milestones against which we can measure progress and use to evaluate the success of the coaching once the journey is completed, when we can celebrate how far the coachee has come. Let's look in more detail at the process of defining and agreeing a good set of goals with our coachee.

SMART goals

A really good goal should be specific, measurable, achievable, relevant to the coachee's role or personal circumstances, and have time limits and target dates attached. In other words, it should be **SMART**:

Specific
Measurable
Achievable
Relevant
Timed

This well-known acronym, developed by George T Doran in 1981, is now in common usage among workplace managers, who use it to set objectives within performance management systems.

Setting clear and specific goals means coachees can clarify their ideas and focus their efforts, allowing them to allocate their time in a way that promises the best return on this investment and the highest chance of achieving success. SMART goals are a fabulous way of getting coachees mentally prepared for what's ahead and of staying motivated when obstacles appear.

Intrinsic versus extrinsic goals

Another key consideration when setting clear and meaningful goals is to look at whether they are 'extrinsic' or 'intrinsic'. Extrinsic goals relate to external factors such as money, fame, status or things involving validation from others. Intrinsic goals relate to internal factors: our personal growth, health and well-being, relationships with yourself and others. In our lives, most of us aim for a mixture of extrinsic and intrinsic goals: for example, wanting to achieve a certain level of financial reward (extrinsic) plus a sense of personal achievement or security (intrinsic).

As an example, let's think of a student applying to university. Do they talk about it as an intrinsic goal where they want to learn, develop and experience new things, leading to a fulfilling career making a difference in the world, or is their goal more extrinsic, driven by conforming with their peers, pleasing their parents, gaining a prestigious degree or an impressive job? Neither is right or wrong, and in most cases a student's motivations are likely to be a mixture of both. It is worth noting that we can be intrinsically motivated to pursue extrinsic goals. For example, the desire to provide financial security and a good standard of living for your family (extrinsic) may be driven by a deeply held personal value (intrinsic).

While both intrinsic and extrinsic goals have value within our lives, goals driven by a strong level of intrinsic motivation, closely linked to our personal strengths and values and of real personal significance, have been associated with higher levels of success, satisfaction and well-being than working towards goals with primarily extrinsic motivations.

The organisation Gallup has researched this extensively. They report that when using their Clifton-Strengths, 'people are more confident and more likely to achieve their goals. They're more likely to report having ample energy, feeling well-rested, being happy, smiling or laughing a lot, learning something interesting, and being treated with respect. And they're less likely to report experiencing worry, stress, anger, sadness or physical pain.'

Approach and avoidance goals

It is always important to think about how goals are phrased, and I would suggest that we try to keep them positive and forward looking – 'approach goals'. These focus on achieving a positive outcome, goals that we work *towards*, while 'avoidance goals' focus more on what we *don't* want, on what we want to prevent, avoid or stop happening. If we return to Nigel, our previous coachee who was unhappy with shift work, his goal framed as an avoidance goal might be to stop working shifts, whereas his goal framed as an approach goal could be to focus on achieving a nine-to-five position.

Positively reframing avoidance goals to become approach goals is an important part of inspirational goal setting. We are often more motivated to work towards a goal about achieving something positive or pleasurable, than by a focus that is simply the avoidance of something negative.

Here are three examples to demonstrate how an avoidance goal can be reframed as an approach goal.

AVOIDANCE GOAL ⟶	APPROACH GOAL
'I want to stop feeling stuck at work.'	'I want to explore wider career progression opportunities.'
'I want to avoid being in debt at the end of the month.'	'I want to be in credit at the end of the month.'
'I want to learn to stop losing my temper when under pressure.'	'I want to learn to remain calm under pressure.'

Setting the goals

In this first section about goal setting, we have started to define goals, and come to understand which goal types are more likely to bring about successful outcomes. I now offer the *what-why-when* question formula and framework which I have found to be successful with most coachees.

EXERCISE: What-why-when questions

In this exercise we provide a handy goal-setting template for goal planning that I have used for years to help people define goals which are clear, challenging but achievable. Each question, for each goal, should be answered in response to the specific nature of that goal, but also within the wider context of the bigger picture and overall dream.

	What	Why	When
	What will you achieve?	*Why is this a good goal for you now?*	*When will you achieve it by?*
Goal 1:			
Goal 2:			
Goal 3:			

When we later move on to start discussing the ideas and commitments that will help us finalise our action plan, we will then be adding an additional element to our three-fold question structure, *what-why-when*, to capture the *how*.

10
Question 8 (Goals)

Can you identify some milestones to mark your progress along the way?

I have encouraged you to conceptualise and then agree to goals that are stretching but also feel achievable; other coaches may encourage their coachees to aim far higher, pushing them to 'reach for the stars'. There is no single right way of setting the perfect goal, it depends on both the coach and the coachee. Some coachees may find a hugely ambitious goal inspiring, but for others it is terrifying; some respond best to big challenges, and others to small steps, breaking goals down into bite-sized chunks, each day moving just a little bit, but always moving forward.

However motivating our aspirations and goals, achieving them can still seem distant and far away. Sometimes the journey may appear overly challenging, making the goals look unattainable, so when a coachee wants to make a big life change or achieve a substantial goal, it can be helpful to break this process down into a series of smaller steps or milestones. There are several benefits to doing this:

- It can help plot a clear pathway from the present to the future.

- It can keep us on track so that we can easily see if we are falling behind or going off course.

- It gives us opportunities to celebrate success along the way, which can motivate us to continue.

When I first started writing this book, I set myself the goal of completing a first draft by the end of the summer. This target, positively framed as an approach goal, felt stretching but achievable. I set off enthusiastically, full of intrinsic motivation, but... it didn't happen. Life got in the way. I knew what I wanted to achieve, but I wasn't moving forward. I knew I needed to break the journey into a series of manageable steps, so I decided I would instigate the habit of writing for a set period of time each day, following the example of many successful authors... but this also didn't happen, and I felt increasingly disheartened and low.

I discussed my problem with a colleague who was also writing a book. He had set himself a goal of writing 10,000 words a month. That initially sounded quite daunting, but when I broke it down, it meant around

2,500 words a week, or 500 words a day with two days off a week. That sounded better, but there were still days when even 500 words still felt too much. In the end I decided to write something every day, even if it was just for five minutes. I didn't succeed every single day, but I managed it most days, and often it led to a much longer writing session. Most importantly, it was rarely too daunting for me to get started for the day when I told myself I only needed to do it for five minutes. It was challenging because of all my other commitments, but it also felt achievable, and created the habit of writing every day. I had finally found something that worked for me, and I had a first draft by September.

The challenge for you, as the coach, is to help find a method that works for your coachee. The good news is that you have at hand the best person to know this – your coachee.

Time, quantity and actionable steps

To make the process of defining the steps a little more streamlined, here are three methods that you can use to help your coachee break their goals down into manageable milestones, sometimes referred to as 'digestible chunks'. These methods break the journey down by different categories: by time, by quantity and by actionable steps.

Breaking goals down by time

One effective way to break goals down is to think about how much time can be allocated to them in a day, week or month. For example, if a person's goal is to learn to play the piano, they might aim to devote half an hour a day for practice. If their goal is to increase their fitness, they may decide to devote four hours a week to exercise. For me, it was five minutes of writing a day.

I started writing this book during a series of Covid lockdowns, where most of us were confined to our homes for long periods of time. I began to suffer with back and shoulder strain from spending so much time at a computer, so I decided to carve out time at the end of the working day to doing half an hour of yoga. Building this habit into the rhythm of my day was a useful way of creating measurable and manageable milestones towards my aspirations and goals around health and well-being.

Breaking goals down by quantity

Another effective approach to breaking goals down is by setting a quantity or quota around how much is to be achieved in a day, week or month. If a person's aspiration is to be more well-read, they might set themselves a goal of reading all of Charles Dickens' novels within in a year. This might seem a daunting task when faced with a huge pile of thick books, but they could break it down further and set a goal of reading at least one title a month, and then even further by agreeing a certain number of chapters a week. This was my colleague's approach with his 10,000 words a month.

Breaking goals down by actionable steps

A third way to break a goal down is into a series of actionable steps, moving from the wider aspirations, to creating a broad goal and finally breaking the targets into smaller steps and stages. In an organisational context, these milestones might be the coachee's shorter-term targets or objectives, or the key stages in the delivery of a project; in a personal context, these might be the key phases of the change they are seeking to make.

This approach often works well when considering career goals. When anyone asked my youngest son what he wanted to be when he grew up, his answer was always a teacher. This aspiration began to solidify when he was in sixth form doing his A-levels and considering his university options, and a specific goal emerged: 'I want to be a music teacher in a state secondary school by the time I am twenty-five.' It then became helpful to break this goal into actionable steps which informed his decision making going forward, particularly deciding whether to study music at a conservatoire or a university. His primary ambition was to teach, not to become a performer first and foremost, so this led him to choose a university course, and gaining a music degree became the next stage in the process, and then on to teacher training. Breaking this goal down into clear actionable steps has been helpful in creating a path towards his aspiration of becoming a music teacher.

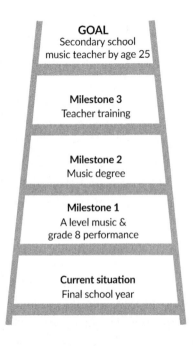

We are going to look at ideas for how to achieve our goals in the next chapter and learn more about identifying actions, tasks and next steps. We are concerned here just about creating mini-milestones to enable your coachee to break their goals into manageable phases, measure progress, keep on track and celebrate success along the way. The key is to make sure there is a strong and well-defined roadmap leading your coachees from their current destination, via a series of stepping stones, to their goals and then their aspirations. These milestones, whether defined by time, quantity or action completed, will be crucial in achieving, recognising and celebrating success.

The goal behind the goal (behind the goal)

When we are creating this roadmap and exploring the links between the coachee's aspirations and goals, you will often find that your coachee's goals, as outlined at the start, will change as they travel through this process. As you delve deeper, you may find there is a larger goal secreted behind the one originally stated.

Here's an example of my own. On New Year's Day last year, I declared that I wanted to get a dog. This is quite a big goal for me, with a significant potential impact on family dynamics.

My husband is, as I've said, an excellent coach himself. He could have declared me unrealistic and reminded me that we already have six children, busy jobs and social lives, and extensive travel plans, plus two cats, two tortoises and an allotment, all of which leave little room to give a dog the time and attention it deserves. Our ancient cat Lollipop, the undisputed queen of the house, would be totally disapproving, and our other cat, Monty, who has a terrible inferiority complex, would probably disappear under the bed, perhaps never to emerge again. Instead he simply asked, 'Why do you want to get a dog?', the perfect reflective coaching question.

'I'm spending too much time sitting and writing and I need to go for a walk every day,' I replied. 'I need a dog to give me an excuse because I can't go walking on my own – that's just weird!'

'OK,' he said, 'tell me more about why you'd like to go walking every day.'

I talked about how it made me feel much better to get some exercise each day, and how I often overcome writing blocks by getting outside and thinking about something else.

'How would we make it work when we are both regularly out all day?' This was a great question, as it helped me see that although there are many benefits, there would also be some logistical challenges to getting a dog.

Then he asked another excellent question: 'It sounds like you want the dog as an excuse to go walking alone every day. What makes it weird to walk on your own? What if it wasn't weird?' This reflective technique is known as 'reframing', enabling me to examine what I have said from a slightly different perspective and questioning the underlying assumptions at play.

I began to understand that there was a bigger goal behind that of getting a dog: what I really wanted was regular exercise. Much as I love them, the desire for a dog was just a distraction goal. My true goal was to go walking for the sake of my physical health and well-being. I was encouraged to explore what it was that I really wanted to achieve and why this was so important to me: What was the goal behind my goal? As I talked it through, I began to realise that there was an aspiration (to improve my health) behind my goal to exercise regularly, which created a milestone activity measured by time (to walk every day), all hidden behind the distraction goal of getting a dog.

Since that realisation, I have made sure to have a walk every single day that I can. I feel much better, and I am happy to report that walking without a dog is lovely, wonderfully peaceful and not actually weird at all!

11
Question 9 (Goals)
To focus on this goal, what else might you need to set aside?

When we are helping our coachees work out timeframes for their goals, we must not forget everything else which currently takes up their time. It is so important to be realistic here, or they will set themselves up for failure because their goal is not achievable, or at least not in the timeframe they have in mind. This final question in our consideration of goals is therefore particularly important question as it explores how we use our time currently, and whether some activities and goals may need to be relinquished for others to flourish. Deciding which goals to focus upon, and which to defer or move away from, can be hard. One tip to help prioritise is to break the goal-setting process down into three distinct stages. Only the best, most relevant and authentic goals will make it through all three stages.

In our first stage, we identify a potential goal through a process of thought, visualisation and discussion. Most of us have many vague goals and plans circling round in our minds at any one time, along the lines of 'One day, I'd love to…' Draw upon them now.

The second stage is to write our goals down, testing them out in more detail and beginning the process of thinking about creating a robust action plan. There seems to be something particularly powerful and satisfying about writing things down where we can see them, be that in words or images, on paper or on screen. Often I find that as a coachee begins the task of finding the right words and ideas to give a tangible form to their goals, this launches the process of creation. Just as the sculptor reveals a statue apparently already hidden within the stone, so this sifting and sorting helps the goal begin to take shape. As the vision begins to clarify, gradually taking on the structure and form of the goal, this actualisation process also helps to clarify whether this is indeed something they want to focus their time and energy on achieving; often they will find that it is not.

Some people, like me, love words, so crafting a beautiful goal statement will present a wonderful opportunity for them, challenging themselves to find exactly the right turn of phrase to capture the joy of their vision of the future. Visual people may think in pictures rather than words, and it can work brilliantly to ask some coachees to illustrate their goal through drawing, illustrations or image collation, rather than capturing it in words, following on from the personal vision statement we created earlier. The coachee can keep this physical reminder of their goal close by to motivate themselves, displaying it prominently or carrying it with them in their wallet or phone as a constant reminder. Only the best and strongest goals reach this stage: we have already seen several occasions when goals becomes less alluring once they were examined in detail.

Finally comes the realisation stage. Action follows and we carry out the plan. We commit time, effort and resources, and our goals begin to come to life as we begin to craft them into reality.

Prioritising

When planning their goals, helping our coachees sort out their priorities can provide a good opportunity to ask some truly reflective coaching questions, holding up a mirror to raise your coachee's awareness of how they use the most valuable commodity of all – their time. You may find that a discussion helping them to prioritise tasks according to the relative importance and urgency of all the activities they undertake is useful.

EXERCISE: The Eisenhower Matrix

A good exercise is to ask your coachee to list all the things they do and the ways they spend their time currently and plot them on this grid, sometimes referred to as the Eisenhower matrix. It defines four areas in terms of both importance (depicted in the vertical plane) and urgency (depicted in the horizontal plane).

Urgent and important	Not urgent and important
Urgent and not important	Not urgent and not important

The top row represents the important activities. The left quadrant represents the area of things which are both important and urgent, the activities that need to be done first. Top right is those that are important but not urgent and should therefore be scheduled for after the first have been completed.

The bottom row considers the less important areas of life. Ask your coachee to consider how much time they are spending – or maybe wasting – on non-important activities: attending meaningless meetings, getting distracted and allowing interruptions to derail them and take their focus away from working on things which are truly important for them?

The ideal quadrant to focus most of our time is the top right area, where we are prioritising activities which are important but not yet urgent. This is where we are organised and focused, and where our best work gets done. When coachees spend a lot of time in the top left quadrant, it may be because they leave things to the last minute. This can therefore be quite stressful, and is often the result of not spending enough time in the top right hand quadrant, planning and thinking ahead.

The Eisenhower matrix is particularly useful for helping your coachee learn to distinguish what is truly important from what is not (but might feel it because of its urgency) and can often be incredibly illuminating. The matrix is good at revealing a few beautifully simple takeaway points, but it can still be difficult to know how to turn this into an actionable plan. This is where we shall introduce the stop, start and continue plan.

EXERCISE: The stop, start and continue plan

Ask your coachee to consider how they spend their time, and then think about where to place each of these activities in three following areas: stop, start and continue:

The key takeaways for anyone completing the exercise are:

What could they **stop** doing?	These are activities which are stealing their time.
	What will happen to these activities if they stop doing them?
	What will the impact be? If the impact is small, then that is a good sign that an activity can be stopped.
	Are they focusing on goals which no longer work for them?
	Have they got into habits which no longer serve them well?
What could they **start** doing?	What are they not doing at the moment, but could benefit from starting to do? These are things which allow them to maximise 'important and not urgent' activities, such as planning ahead and scheduling their work.
What could they **continue** doing?	These are all those great things which are working well for them currently.
	You may have heard the phrase, 'If it ain't broke, don't fix it!' Sometimes it is important to acknowledge and celebrate what we are already doing right.

Completing this grid is a great exercise to use for yourself as well as being a fantastic coaching tool, particularly when coachees talk about being stressed, overloaded and frustrated.

These two exercises illustrate the power of this powerful prioritisation question: 'To focus on this goal, what else might you need to set aside?' As always, the value is in the discussion, so take your time to create some silence while you work with your coachee to answer this question.

This puts us in a good place to focus on the next area where we start to consider ideas for making things happen.

12
Question 10 (Ideas)
What ideas do you have for how to achieve this goal?

By this stage, your coachee will have created an inspiring vision of their future. You'll have explored the blockages that have until now stood in the way of their aspirations and helped identify some strategies for overcoming them; your coachee will have a clear set of goals, outlined within well-defined and achievable timeframes, and introduced some key milestones to measure their progress. It is now time to start helping them plan the actions that will lead to the achievement of these goals.

'What ideas do you have to achieve this goal?' is the first of a series of questions designed to keep widening their thinking. The exercises and tools provided so far should have left you in a great place for this next stage, where we begin to generate ideas and create plans.

When you ask your coachee this question, the first answers they provide will typically be existing ideas and things that they have previously identified. This is all good and useful, but there is a reason why they haven't yet achieved this goal or employed these strategies and ideas already. Your role now is to encourage them to think outside the box and to come up with some new ones. It's important to be non-judgemental here: we are often quick to dismiss options by saying why things won't work or can't be done, but it is important to resist this temptation. Start by suspending all opinion and setting aside all preconceptions; instead concentrate on working with your coachee to generate a expansive range of options, however outlandish or unlikely they might seem; there will be plenty of time for evaluating their ideas later.

For coachees who like to work creatively, working on a flipchart or whiteboard is often useful. You could encourage your coachees to draw their ideas, generate a mindmap, use different colours and shapes, and simply use the vast expanse of blank space to let the mind wander; there are an increasing number of effective tools online to help capture ideas in similar ways if you are working virtually. By contrast, more pragmatic, systematic or theoretically minded coachees might prefer lists and spreadsheets. Your coachees may appreciate space and time to think about this exercise in advance, so it is a good idea to ask them to consider ideas and actions before your session, to yield a better response and not put them under immediate pressure.

Idea-generation tools

In this section, I provide a number of idea-generation tools that can help you overcome blockages at this stage. They are deliberately totally different from each other: one that resonates and works brilliantly with one coachee may fall totally flat with another, so you can use your judgement about which tool to use, with which coachee, at which time.

Stream of consciousness

The stream of consciousness is a style or technique used successfully by many writers and is essentially a form of focused free-writing. It can help your coachee gain clarity by allowing their thoughts and ideas to flow freely from their brain onto the paper. You can use a stream of consciousness process to create a visual, or just let the words flow and write it down. Whatever works best to capture their thoughts.

This exercise works best when people are not feeling rushed or distracted, so we need to create a calm and relaxed atmosphere. Therefore, this could work well as a homework activity between sessions, to allow your coachee to find a quiet time when they can fully concentrate. It is a great example of creating space for the magic happening in the silence.

EXERCISE: Stream of consciousness

Your coachee should note down their goal at the top of the page – it doesn't matter whether it is a big long-term goal or a shorter-term milestone – and then work through the following process, drawing on work you have done to get to this point:

1. Ask them to start by writing down everything they currently know about the goal: create a picture of the future and how it will look and feel.

2. Next they note down all the details of the current situation. Describe the bridge between the Mirror of their current reality and the Aspiration and Goals of their future. They could also capture anything that they don't know and would need to find out. Where are the gaps?

3. Now they are in the flow, ask them to continue by recording what they would like to do next, and what they would like to happen. How would they like to move forward and what would they like to do? Encourage them not to feel constrained at this point, but to think of an ideal world where barriers are reduced and obstacles can be overcome; remind them of the magic wand. Encourage them to write down all their ideas, whether big and small, easily achievable or terrifyingly challenging.

4. Finally, ask them to finish by adding anything else that they are currently thinking and feeling. While they are 'in the zone', this is an opportunity to get whatever is floating around in their head out into the world.

This stream of consciousness methodology is about enabling our coachees to get their thoughts written down on paper. Sometimes people are quite surprised by what comes out once they get started. It is important not to be interrupted, because this works best when people become so immersed in the flow of the exercise that they appear to be writing from their subconscious, tapping into a deeper energy that can be illuminating and revealing. The object of this exercise is to get past the initial block that can often inhibit some coachees, then step back and discuss what has emerged. You will know this has worked well if they surprise themselves with the results.

As a coach, you play an important role here in keeping the process going if they get stuck, by asking questions to stimulate further thought, but try to keep your input to prompting, not leading or influencing. By this stage in our journey, you fully understand the power of holding the silence, but you will need to learn to distinguish between silence that represents insightful thought, and when it means they have hit a brick wall. If it is the latter, you could consider one of the other exercises below to reignite their thinking.

Storyboarding

Storyboarding is the process of capturing numerous elements of a journey, each in an unlimited amount of detail, and is a technique borrowed from the world of filmmaking. The aim is to create a visual journey, so your coachee can see how ideas interact and connect; this is helpful in thinking about sequencing and planning. Sticky notes, real or virtual, are a fantastic aid here: I use them all the time in my coaching and training as they are colourful, versatile and easy to move around to visualise changes. This detailed planning enables numerous possibilities to be considered, assessed, celebrated or then discarded, assisting in the advanced recognition of any potential obstacles or barriers along the way.

EXERCISE: Storyboarding

- Ask your coachee to take a few minutes to write some initial ideas on individual sticky notes; this can be done virtually using an online tool, or using real stickies when face-to-face. Their answers don't have to be fully conceived or well thought-out ideas, they can be random thoughts, quotes, pictures and even just words.

- Once they have a pile of sticky notes, they can start to arrange them into in a logical order or flow; this can be done on a table, flipchart, whiteboard or screen. Encourage them to move them around as much as necessary, first one way, then another, to explore how each change impacts on the flow and feeling of the overall sequence.

- Organising and displaying ideas sequentially can help us see new relationships between different aspects, identify connections and generate new ideas about how to move forward. It can help to establish whether there is a natural flow or process to their ideas, and will reveal the innate timeline of the journey as you find one element needs to be achieved before another can be attempted.

Mood boards

A mood board is a collage of ideas, captured via words, images, fabrics etc or a combination of various media; it can be created physically or digitally. Artists and designers frequently use them in the early stages of a creative project: collating material to begin to build a vision of the desired future can help inspire both creator and client. It also facilitates the sharing of initial ideas and thoughts at an early stage in a physical and tangible form so that they can be seen and better understood by others, enabling any necessary changes or clarifications to be agreed at this early stage. Inspired by the mood board content, the designer can then produce original coherent designs in line with the wider brief and informed by mood board feedback. It is a great concept that we can borrow and use in our coaching, enabling our coachees to collect thoughts, ideas and inspirations in one place, clustered around a central aspiration or goal. We have already touched on using variations of this idea when depicting goals and aspirations, so you may already have a mood board to work with here.

EXERCISE: The mood board

Your coachee starts by writing their aspirations, goals or targets on a large sheet (at the top or in the centre). Then encourage them to collect pictures, images, colours and words which encapsulate or symbolise this goal for them. Encourage them to tap into their own creativity, and you will find out what inspires them. Can they explore their goal through music, painting, photography, sculpture, textiles or even smells and memories? Whatever and wherever they find inspiration. Letting their creative juices flow, in whatever way they find most inspires them, can encourage fresh thinking to emerge.

Two additional techniques: The Magic Wand and the AWE question

In addition to the exercises just covered, there are two additional techniques that can be used at any stage of the coaching process, but may be particularly valuable here: the concept of the magic wand and the so-called 'AWE question'.

1. Now could be the perfect time to reintroduce the metaphorical 'magic wand' that we called upon earlier to strip away constrains and concerns, freeing the imagination to dream. Ask your coachee what they would do if they could wave this wand once again, especially if the concept struck a chord with them.

2. The 'AWE question' stands for *And What Else...?*
   and is named by Michael Bungay Stanier as 'the
   best coaching question in the world'; I would
   be inclined to agree. You can use this question
   at any stage of your coaching and it will always
   add value. Whenever you feel there is more to
   be said, simply asking, 'And what else...?' may
   be all that is needed to prompt your coachee
   to keep talking and take the discussion a little
   deeper.

As you work through this Ideas section, do not be
tempted to rush. It takes time to explore ideas, and
that's why utilising one or two of these exercises
can work so well as they add variety, energy and
movement to your sessions. When we are looking
to generate a wide range and breadth of ideas, we
often need first to lay out again the obvious options
and those considered in the past, before they can
then come up with new and potentially more interesting ones. Many of these will be nonstarters and
never get off the drawing board, but it is important
to keep going: we only need one really good idea to
capture their imagination, fire them with enthusiasm and bring that bridge to their destination more
into sight.

I have presented a range of exercises, tools and techniques so you can find one or two which work well for
you and your coachee, to stimulate fresh ideas which
we can then turn into a tangible plan, in the fifth and

final stage of the MAGIC process, in which we will begin to widen the thought process even further, to consider how your coachee might draw on external resources and enlist the help of others.

13
Question 11 (Ideas)
Where could you go for help, support, advice and inspiration?

In 1675, Sir Isaac Newton acknowledged the debt he owed to the ideas of others who had come before him, paying tribute with the words, 'If I have seen a little further, it is by standing upon the shoulders of giants.' I love this quote and here it helps remind us that we don't always have to 'reinvent the wheel' when making plans to achieve our own goals.

Much of what we do is based on, guided by and made possible by the experiences, experimentation and achievements of those who have gone before. Our most significant successes can build from this foundation of established knowledge, pushing boundaries and stretching ideas to see how things can be done differently and better going forward. However, your coachee won't be alone if they sometimes demonstrate resistance to doing this. This was articulated perfectly by the author Douglas Adams when he wrote 'Human beings, who are almost unique in having the ability to learn from the experience of others, are also remarkable for their apparent disinclination to do so.' I know that I have demonstrated such resistance at times, wanting to do everything all by myself, but I really do believe there is great value to be gained by seeking inspiration from others.

This chapter outlines how to assist your coachees as they work through how and where they could seek inspiration and support from others. Some great questions to open this discussion and explore this area more fully could include:

- Who could you talk to about your plans?

- Who has valuable experience from which you can learn?

- What have other people done to achieve this goal?

- Who do you think could assist you in finding a way achieve your aspirations and goals?

- Who do you think could inspire you in this challenge?

- What other resources can you draw on?

The skill you are trying to encourage within your coachee is the ability to judge the right idea for the right situation at the right time. Encourage your coachee to think about their role models and other successful people who have been successful in their chosen field or niche. What path did they follow to achieve their success? Where could your coachee research what others have done? What can they borrow and how can they learn from others, and apply old ideas to new situations? Where can they go for inspiration?

Tapping into other perspectives

Here is a great coaching exercise you can use at this stage in the process.

EXERCISE: Musical chairs

This is an exercise aimed at helping your coachee shift their perspective by imaginatively tapping into the perspectives of others.

Start by asking your coachee to think of several different people who may have a stake in their goals or something to add; their answers will be totally personal and situation-specific. In a work context they may choose key stakeholders, their manager, a respected colleague or a customer. In a personal context, they may choose their partner, parents, children or friends.

They could choose people in public life whose achievements or opinions they respect. They might explore Edward de Bono's 'six thinking hats' concept and try putting on, metaphorically or even literally, a series of hats representing various viewpoints, one of logic and facts, optimism, playing the devil's advocate, feelings and emotion, creativity and management. The characters selected are totally flexible; I have seen the exercise work with the coachee using fictional characters, superheroes or even historical characters. The purpose is simply to consider at least two or three different perspectives, but you can be flexible here and see what works best for them.

Whichever alternative viewpoints have been selected, the coachee should ask themself a series of broad questions based around exploring these perspectives:

- What would their parents do? What would their children do?

- What would their manager do? What would their role model do?

- What would their best friend do? What would their rival do?

- What would a successful author, artist, inventor or influencer do?

- What would they tell themselves to do, if they were looking from the outside in?

As you ask your coachee to view their situation from the different perspectives of the people they have chosen, it can be useful to illustrate this imaginative shift by physically moving so they are literally sitting in a different chair for each perspective, but it can also be done purely as a conceptual exercise. As they move to each chair, physically or metaphorically, ask them to imagine the situation from the perspective of this individual and describe the help, advice and support they might offer. Some people love this exercise and

find it stimulating and energising; others are a bit
bemused by it! Either way, it may prove to be a useful
addition to your coaching toolbox.

This is a powerful exercise and can increase empathy
through an enhanced understanding of the perspectives of others, as well as also often provoking and
inspiring new ideas and fresh approaches. It is also
possible that your coachee feels a bit disheartened
or is facing failure or rejection. This is an occasion
when considering the experiences of others can also
offer real value and release. There are many inspirational stories about those who have persevered and
achieved success against the odds or after setbacks
and rejections, and these examples can be used to
help encourage your coachee to keep going when the
going gets tough.

I've introduced several different exercises so far, with
more to come, but I am not suggesting you use every
exercise with every coachee. My aim has been to offer
you a variety of different coaching tools, to enable you
to choose the right activity at the right time for the
right coachee. Some may have completely resonated
with you and others not at all, but I hope you have
found a few with which you can become firm friends
to assist you in your role as a coach.

14
Question 12 (Ideas)
How can you evaluate these ideas?

If you and your coachee have been following the MAGIC coaching trajectory thus far, you will by now have generated a long list of potential ideas that could help them move forward in achieving their goals. With this next stage, we will move on to evaluating these new ideas. Which ideas are potential winners? Which will be assigned to the no-go category? Which should be put aside for later? To assign our ideas to these three basic categories, we need first to consider the broader question, 'How can you evaluate these ideas?'

Two idea analysis tools

Here are two simple exercises, both of which will help your coachee evaluate their ideas and work out which are the best to take forward.

EXERCISE: Pluses and Minuses

This is essentially a simple analysis of the pros and cons of each idea using a tried and tested exercise that is widely used and hugely popular, rightly so; sometimes the simplest methods really are the best. As always, the value is in the conversation, so slow down and take your time, and remember the value of silence.

Start by creating a table or spreadsheet with four columns:

Potential idea	Plus points	Minus points	Star rating ☆☆☆☆☆

Your coachee should list a selection of their ideas in the left-hand column. Encourage them to pick some of the more 'off the wall' ideas as well as the obviously strong candidates; thinking through the broader strengths and weaknesses of these other ideas, even if at first they seem bizarre or unlikely, will sometimes reveal a surprise contender or even lead to further new ideas as these hidden gems get refined. I tend to suggest they start with one or two of their favourite ideas, one they don't like as much, and the strangest or most outlandish idea, to see if there could be some merit in that too.

Ask your coachee to think of at least one plus point (a strength), and one minus point (a weakness), for each idea. They may find that the strengths of a particular idea come thick and fast, or equally it might be the weaknesses. Prompt your coachee to consider the ideas from different angles and encourage them to question their thinking and challenge any assumptions or preconceptions. Is that unconventional idea really so outlandish after all? Is there a way to make it work?

To help them think differently, you could challenge them to remove the emotion and think purely logically: What does their head say? Then challenge them to remove the logic and think purely emotionally: What does their heart say?

Once they have completed this questioning process for each of the ideas on their list, go through the list and ask them to award a star rating to each, based on your discussion and their comments. The higher the stars score, the better the idea.

This exercise works particularly well for people with a leaning towards thinking and analysing in a systematic and logical way, but even for those to whom it does not come so naturally, this methodical approach to assessing each option in turn can be extremely useful. To make it more visual, you could also add elements of colour coding to the exercise or create it on a spreadsheet.

Our second tool is equally powerful and another great way to plot your coachee's ideas to enable them to prioritise and weigh up each potential option. You can complete this after the 'pluses and minuses' exercise or use it as a standalone activity.

EXERCISE: The-gives-versus-the-gains matrix

Start by asking your coachee to write a selection of their ideas, each one on an individual sticky notes, whether paper or virtual.

Now draw an unpopulated version of the grid below on a whiteboard, paper or screen.

GAINS →

	LOW REWARD	HIGH REWARD
HIGH EFFORT		
LOW EFFORT		

GIVES ↑

The matrix calls for each idea to be assessed according to two criteria:

- The **gives**
- The **gains**

On the vertical axis, we have the gives: How much will they have to give to make this option work? In other words, what is the cost, in terms of money, time, effort and other opportunities lost? Some ideas and options will require a large investment of time, effort and perhaps money; the give score here is high. Others will be easy, simple and quick to implement; here the give score is lower.

On the horizontal axis, we have the gains element: Potentially how much could they gain by pursuing this option, in terms of time, satisfaction, happiness, money or success? What are the rewards? How far will it move them towards their goal and how quickly? Some ideas offer huge benefits and could reap great rewards; these have a high gains score.

For others, the gains may be negligible and the benefits slight; here the gains score will be low.

Working with your coachee, take up the sticky notes and start to position them on the matrix where they fit best, talking through each idea as you go. Some ideas will sit firmly in one area, if the give or the gain is particularly high, while others will sit nearer the middle.

When you have helped your coachee plot their various options and ideas, stand back and evaluate the grid as a whole. Make sure they are happy with where everything sits. It is fine to keep moving things around, as all ideas are relative to each other.

Now consider this slightly expanded matrix. Having decided where each idea is curently placed, now we need to decide how to use this information. Our ideas can now be divided into 'timewasters' and 'distractions', 'stars' and 'easy wins'. Has this changed how your coachee views some of their ideas?

	GAINS	
	LOW REWARD ——→ HIGH REWARD	
HIGH EFFORT	**Timewasters** High effort, low reward Top Tip: Don't be a busy fool (as my granny used to say)!	**Stars** High effort, high reward Top Tip: Well worth the effort but don't embark on too many of these at once as it could be overwhelming.
LOW EFFORT	**Distractions** Low effort, low reward Top Tip: Don't get distracted by the low effort required by these tasks, if they don't deliver rewards either.	**Easy wins** Low effort, high reward Top Tip: What's not to like? Tick these off your list with a sense of satisfaction!

(GIVES — vertical axis label, from LOW EFFORT up to HIGH EFFORT)

Consider with your coachee the ideas that require high effort. If the potential gains are low, these ideas may not be worth the high effort, whereas if the gains are high, the necessary investment of time and effort may be justified. Help them evaluate the resources needed, the time, money or energy required. Pick some 'low-hanging fruit': if there are high gains to be made for relatively little effort, these ideas can be a great place to start.

Encourage your coachee to question their thinking and analyse each idea as broadly as possible. If your coachee says things like, 'That won't work,' now is the time to challenge them. How do they know that? Where's the data to back that up? Ask them additional questions about ideas which seem vague. Can they add any more details? Does this help give clarity, or maybe generate even more options and ideas for them?

The purpose of this discussion is to assess which actions have the highest potential payback and therefore where your coachee should best invest their valuable time and effort. This process should generate a robust list of tangible and workable ideas in which your coachee can have real confidence and hopes for success.

___

As we now reach the end of this Ideas stage of the MAGIC Methodology, we have helped our coachee generate a good range of credible, exciting ideas to start to work with. Now it is time to turn our attention to creating a plan, moving from 'What *could* you do?' to our final stage which addresses the crucial issue, 'What *will* you do?'

15

Question 13 (Commitments)

What's your plan?

We are really moving forward now as we come to the fifth and final stage of the MAGIC Methodology. This is a particularly exciting stage as we move from considering what the coachee potentially *could* do to the crucial stage of determining what they *will* do. Our coachees should be feeling motivated and inspired, as we begin to work with them on how to turn their ideas generated so far into a robust plan, with milestones, actions, priorities and dates.

The generation of an actionable and tangible plan is one of the most important outputs of an effective coaching session. We know the value is in the discussion, and how stimulating, invigorating and even provocative these conversations can be so it is important to encourage your coachee to take their time over this stage and talk through their thought process. Have the confidence to hold the silence and remember our fundamental principle as a coach: *ask, don't tell.* It will be your coachee who will be responsible for actioning everything that is decided, so it needs to be their plan and they need to feel a strong sense of ownership.

Earlier on our MAGIC journey, when asking our coachees Question 7: 'Can you create clear goals, achievable within a realistic timeframe?', we used a simple template to capture clear goals via the *what-why-when* question format. Now that we are ready to create a plan, we can update this template to add our final element, as mentioned earlier. This fourth component to the three-question structure will become their plan of action: *How* will they achieve this goal? Some people like to keep their plan short and succinct, while others prefer a comprehensive spreadsheet with dependencies, resources and a high level of detail. In my coaching business, we have used this format with coachees for many years, but please feel free to adapt it to suit your own personal coaching style and each individual coachee.

A template for action

Goal 1: Your goal here

What	Why	When
What is your goal?	*Why is this a good goal for you now?*	*When will you achieve it by?*
What will you achieve?	How does it link to your wider aspirations and goals?	Set a specific deadline for each milestone along the way.

How

How will you achieve it? What's your plan?

List the key milestones along the way and the activities you will undertake to achieve them.

Milestone 1:	Your actions, plans and priorities
Target date:	
Milestone 2:	Your actions, plans and priorities
Target date:	
Milestone 3:	Your actions, plans and priorities
Target date:	

Begin by asking your coachee to write their goal at the top. This will be one of the goals we identified with Question 7 ('Can you create clear goals, achievable within a realistic timeframe?') so make sure it is well-defined and specific, clarifying the links to their wider goals and aspirations with target dates and deadlines. In our earlier work on this question, we helped our coachee learn how to break things down into smaller steps or milestones; these too can be listed on the form. Now we can begin to formulate the specific actions and plans which will enable them to achieve these milestones and move toward their goals.

Work with your coachee to build a list of all the activities that need to happen to reach each milestone successfully. Use the ideas you worked on together in the previous section, reviewing the pluses and minuses you listed for each, and considering which ideas will produce the *highest gain* for the *lowest give*. The more specific they can be, the better.

Generating plans

You can create plans outlining how to achieve your goals and milestones using several different approaches, depending on the nature of the goal and the associated action plan; here are some ideas to help. Just as we broke our goals down into milestones, dividing them up by a different measurable and definable quantity, so we can use the same concept in the process of planning how to achieve these goals.

Deadlines: We may build our plan around a series of daily, weekly, monthly or quarterly deadlines, deciding where we would like to be at each stage and how much we want to move forward each time until we reach our target date.

Time: We could create a plan which stipulates how much time we will devote to working on our goals.

Themes: Alternatively, you could break a goal into 'themes', each mapping a different element of your goal. Some of these you will work on simultaneously, while others will be sequentially dependent upon each other.

Quantity: We might commit ourselves to achieving certain numbers along the way.

My personal target this year is to achieve an average count per day of 7,000 steps. I don't mind how long this takes me in a day, when I do it, or whether I walk or run to achieve it, but I am finding that this is an achievable and enjoyable target. Some days I easily track 10,000 steps or more, and other days I am desk-bound and struggle to achieve even a quarter of this, but as long as the average overall remains at 7,000, then I feel that I am on track.

Having decided how they would like to indicate these milestones, they now need to generate some form of sequence. Some milestones and activities will be of a higher priority than others, so ask them to decide how significant and urgent each item is. Which activities will they do first? If they only have a chance to carry out one or two activities, which ones will be the most important? You could ask them to rate the activities as high, medium or low priority. As they work through the activities in their plan, they can readjust the priorities at any stage.

Good questions to ask here include:

- Which actions are the highest priority?

- What resources or support will you need to achieve them?

- Are there other steps that need to be undertake first?

- Who else may be affected by your actions?

- How will you overcome potential obstacles and barriers?

- What can you do to enhance your chance of success?

Some coachees will find it helpful to start at the end goal and work backwards, identifying key milestones and deadlines in reverse; Scott Murphy calls this 'back to the future' planning. One of the benefits of doing this is that by the time you get back to the first milestone, it should feel contextualised. They can easily see how the first stage is part of a bigger journey, and where their first steps will lead them. Others will find it easier to start with the present and work on identifying just their first few steps initially, leaving the details of the more distant stages until nearer the time.

Some coachees might find it helpful to create a visualisation of their plan, a road map outlining their path to their destination with the key milestones indicated along the way. As an example, here is my real plan for the steps toward the publication of this book, with the key milestones and activities organised into themes. At the time, I also included target dates for each activity.

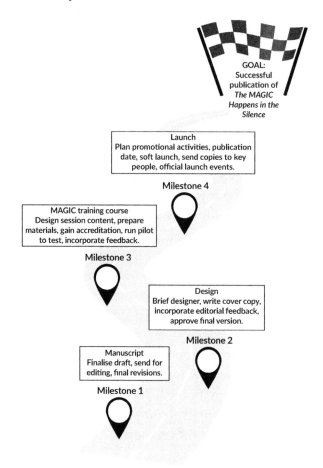

Overcoming barriers and obstacles

By this stage on our systematic journey through the MAGIC Methodology, we have spent a significant amount of time helping our coachee identify, clarify and prepare to achieve their aspirations and goals. Although we hope that they will now be keen and motivated to begin, it is still common for people to feel nervous of starting. To address this understandable hesitation and to have the greatest chance of success, it is valuable to consider the barriers and obstacles that could arise along the journey, and create strategies to overcome or minimise these.

Much of our earlier work around questions such as 'What makes this important to you now?' (Question 3) and 'What has stopped you crossing this bridge before now?' (Question 6) will prove invaluable once again, bringing additional depth to our current considerations of Question 12. We may need to revisit some of the factors identified in those discussions to make sure that the same issues don't rear their heads again. What will be different this time? If we haven't identified what has previously stopped our coachee from progressing, then there is a strong chance that the same issue could stop them again. As we have discussed, it isn't usually time which stops us achieving our goals, although that will always be a factor in our busy lives. It is more likely to be a lack of clarity, the wrong goal or fear of the unknown.

EXERCISE: What lies ahead?

One effective way of managing this discussion is to confront these potential barriers and obstacles up front. By identifying these at the planning stage, we can build in strategies, solutions, safeguards and alternatives to ensure they do not derail our journey.

To do this most effectively, I like to create a simple table with four columns.

1. In the first column, ask your coachee to list any potential obstacles or barriers to success that they think could arise.

2. In the next, ask them to evaluate the likelihood of this possibility occurring; consider the likelihood on a scale from low to high.

3. The third column considers the scale of the impact it would have on the plan if the event under consideration were to come about; this can be measured from one (negligible/minor) to five (catastrophic).

4. In the final column, the coachee should brainstorm avoidance steps, techniques and mitigation strategies that you could use to reduce the likelihood of these events occurring, diminish the scale of the impact if they do, and minimise the chance of these barriers throwing the journey off course.

Potential barrier/ obstacles	Likelihood of occurrence (unlikely/ possible/ likely/certain)	Scale of impact if it occurs 1 (minor)– 5 (catastrophic)	Possible solutions

Creating a solid and workable plan is a key outcome from a successful coaching session, and considering barriers and obstacles is an essential part of this process. Some barriers and obstacles will be external, perhaps a lack of time, money or resources; others will be internal, perhaps a lack of confidence or skills. Articulating these potential roadblocks at the planning stage and identifying a range of workable solutions, can help increase a coachee's sense of control and confidence. If or when they do arise, the coachee is well prepared, with some solutions ready to go.

Now we have a robust plan, with contingencies and mitigation strategies built in, the end is in sight. We are therefore ready to move onto our next question, where we will focus on clarifying the first few steps.

16
Question 14 (Commitments)

What is the first thing you will do to start you on your way?

In the seminal Taoist text, *Tao Te Ching*, written thousands of years ago, appears the familiar Chinese proverb that 'a journey of a thousand miles begins with a single step.' A similar sentiment is found in ancient Greek philosophy, where variations of the proverb 'well begun is half done' are cited by both Plato and Aristotle. These wise words recognise the importance not just of getting started, but of starting well.

Question 14: 'What is the first thing you will do to start you on your way?' is therefore hugely important psychologically and in terms of establishing a sense of momentum, and yet sometimes getting going can be the hardest bit of all. As your coachee leaves your session, it is important that their first steps are clear and straightforward, with an immediate and visible impact. If they can achieve tangible early successes, however small, their momentum is so much more likely to continue.

The MAGIC questioning arc can be used in a single session or spread over several sessions, depending on the nature of the coaching you are providing. Sometimes you might ask all fifteen questions in one session, other times you could spend the whole period exploring a single MAGIC section, or even just one question. Regardless of how much has been covered that day, I would recommend that, at the end, you always jump forward to this final section, Commitment, so that your coachee leaves every session with some tangible next steps and an agreed plan of action.

Here are three useful top tips to use with your coachee to help them get started:

- Make the first step totally specific and look to eliminate any uncertainty or vagueness.

- Pick some 'quick wins' to do first – actions that are 'low gives' but 'high gains', low effort and high rewards – to help motivate them with some early success.

- Encourage them to stop procrastinating and trying to make everything perfect before they make a start. Just take that first step, however small.

Increasing motivation and commitment

When discussing the implementation of the coachee's plans, we will sometimes sense some hesitation or nervousness; if this is the case, I would suggest that it needs investigating.

A great tactic to explore this is to ask is what we call a 'scaling' question, where we ask them to give a rating to their commitment or enthusiasm. For example, you could ask, 'How committed are you to this plan, on a scale of one to ten?' What we are gently asking here, without the coachee feeling threatened or disbelieved, is 'Are you actually going to do any of this?'

If your coachee responds with a high commitment level, maybe eight or nine, that's great! Move right along! If their commitment level is low, then we need to examine why. Coachees, and coaches, often get really fired up and enthusiastic during a session; the motivation soars and the commitment feels (and likely is) totally heartfelt at this point. If their commitment isn't sufficiently high now, as you are approaching the end of your super inspiring coaching session and when you would expect enthusiasm to be at its peak, then it is likely that little will happen afterwards when real-life comes crowding back in. Coachees will some-times have to be resilient and motivated to carve out the time required to act and overcome barriers, and confronting that can be quite intimidating.

These are some possible reasons for low commitment levels:

- The goals, the timings or the plans are not right.

- The goals or ideas have come from other people, from work colleagues, friends, family or even from you, but not truthfully from the coachee themself.

- On occasion, there may still be another obstacle, difficulty, hurdle or hesitation that they haven't yet shared. This could be an external barrier, caused by pressures and forces from outside, or internal, existing within their own mind. Again, the challenge is to help your coachee reveal and explore these hidden blocks.

- Finally, they may already feel that they have missed key milestones or they are questioning their ability to meet the targets they have agreed, as low self-esteem and confidence bites. These can certainly all result in lost enthusiasm and must be addressed.

In my experience, we achieve our best results through the habits and behaviours that we practice regularly, not through exquisitely crafted written plans, looking marvellous but gathering dust, or through spectacular one-off bursts of frantic activity followed by long periods of stasis. We move towards excellence by creating compelling and inspiring goals, adopting beneficial habits that we build into our everyday lives, and then working on our goals at least every week, if not every day. I have seen this to be true repeatedly in my own family. I have mentioned that my youngest son is a musician. Time and again, musicians hear the same lines:

'You're so lucky to be good at music… it's such a gift.'

'It's practice,' a musician will reply.

'I wish I could play like you do,' people say.

'It's practice,' the musician replies.

'You're so talented,' people will say.

'It's practice,' they reply. 'We practise every day'.

It's the same with sport, cookery, writing, art, public speaking and many, many other activities. We may be blessed with a natural aptitude, we might find some things easier than others do, but ultimately success comes through hard work and practice, through the regular execution of excellent habits. The key coaching message is that if at first they don't succeed, we should encourage our coachees to try, try again. They will learn something every time they try: persistence pays off, and hard work, resilience, tenacity and determination are the biggest contributors to helping us achieve our goals.

Here are my ten top tips you can share with your coachee for increasing their motivation and commitment and helping them to stay on track through change and uncertainty:

1. Write down your goals and display them prominently, so you can see them every day.

2. Break big tasks down into smaller milestones.

3. Celebrate every success, however small.

4. Put goals, actions and deadlines in your calendar or on your phone, with alerts and/or reminders. (I do this a lot and I cannot overstate how useful I find it – my own PA, secretary and cheerleader, all in my pocket and ready to help when I try to remember where I am meant to be and why!)

5. Share your aspirations, goals, ideas and commitments with a handful of supportive and positive people who can act as your coaching buddies.

6. Focus on just one or two things at a time. Don't overcommit yourself and risk the disappointment, to yourself and others, of under delivering.

7. Be consistent. Work on your plans regularly, ideally every day, even if just for five minutes. Tiny steps soon add up.

8. Don't berate yourself or give up if you miss a deadline. Pick yourself up and keep on going.

9. Remember *why* you're doing what you're doing and remind yourself often, making links to wider aspirations and goals.

10. Make yourself accountable, even if only to yourself.

This last tip is an interesting one, with slight overtones of using the proverbial 'stick' as well as the 'carrot'. To assist your coachees in developing new habits, in many ways one of the hardest for all of us, remind them that you will review their progress at your next meeting. Reflective coaching is a cyclical, ongoing process. When I meet a coachee for a follow-up session, the first thing I do is review the commitments they made last time, celebrating the achievements and exploring any barriers and obstacles they might have encountered. My coachees often confess that it was the knowledge that I would be checking in with them that motivated them to keep going when they felt disheartened or demotivated (as we all do occasionally!): 'I made sure I did it because I knew you'd be asking me,' is a common refrain in my sessions. Although as coaches we aim to promote and encourage self-responsibility and self-motivation, the truth is that people often turn to a coach because they feel that, at that stage, they need that additional element of accountability to someone else.

Regular reviews are a crucial element of effective coaching and being held accountable in this way is a key benefit of a coaching relationship; helping your coachee make the gradual and supported transition from this extrinsic motivation towards a more intrinsic self-motivation is a key goal in maintaining the benefits long after your coaching has finished. The deceptively simple question, 'What is the first thing you will do to start you on your way?' sets the wheels in motion.

17
Question 15 (Commitments)
What are your biggest takeaways from today's session?

A key skill in coaching is knowing how to bring each coaching session to an end in a constructive and positive way, with your coachees feeling enthused and empowered. After you have clarified with your coachee the first few steps that they will take to get started, I would then recommend that you pull the session together with a succinct and tangible summary of the key takeaway points; 'What are your biggest takeaways from today's session?' is the question I use at the end of every coaching session. Closing in this way allows your coachee to reflect on the significant points of the session, while also enabling you to gather valuable feedback for yourself.

This moment of quiet consideration and review can become quite inspirational as they reflect on the bridge they have crossed to reach their current position, now able to see the journey that lies ahead; it can also highlight the most valuable lessons they have learned that will facilitate their future success. As always, we let our coachee speak first and share their thoughts and reflections, but this is also a fantastic time for you to acknowledge the growth you have seen in them and help celebrate the progress they have made. You may have seen shifts in mindset, enhanced self-awareness and self-reflection, and stronger analytical and assessment skills. The coachee might not even be aware of these subtle but significant transitions and accomplishments, and your observations can be illuminating and motivational for them, strengthening and supporting their budding self-confidence and belief.

If you are bringing a whole coaching programme to an end, you could allocate much more time to this important question, perhaps even a whole session, and this can be an excellent time to repeat some of the exercises undertaken at the start of your coaching and compare their responses then and now. For example, this is a great moment to revisit the Magic Wheel exercise we completed within our Question 1 discussions, to visually demonstrate their progress.

In my early days as a coach, one of the things I found hardest was bringing a session to an end without feeling as if I was being rude, rushing the coachee or closing them down. Some coachees will be aware of the approaching end and may themselves conclude the session without prompting, saying things like, 'I know that our time is almost up.' If the coachee isn't keeping track of time or is too absorbed in the work, it is then your responsibility to draw the session to a close in a careful manner. Doing this skilfully, leaving both your coachee and yourself in a good place, is an important technique to learn, to respect and protect your time and theirs.

As the session draws into the later stages, don't be tempted to open new major topics or to begin discussing an area that you cannot explore fully in the time left available. If the coachee broaches a new subject, it can work well to say, 'I think that exploring this issue may require more time than we have left. Can I suggest that we cover it during our next session?' This shows the coachee that you value their contributions and your mutual boundaries, but also places the subject on the table for the following occasion.

Closing a session

Here are some tips to help manage the time, as you lead into our final question and prepare to end your session.

It might sound obvious, but the first tip is to make sure you have clear and direct sight of a clock; position the clock in the same direction as your coachee so you can glance at the time without having to look away from your coachee. Worrying about the time can be distracting, and if you look at your watch, however discreetly, it can appear rude. Other tips include slightly changing your tone of voice or body language, perhaps speaking slightly faster, leaning forward or sitting up straighter, to create a change in the energy.

I have suggested ways in which you can gently flag the approaching end of the session, in both your questions and your behaviour, but if your coachee still keeps talking, you may need to be a little more direct, because it is important that you close the session properly. You could say something like, 'Our time is nearly up so we will need to stop here. Before we finish, I'd like to ask you one more question. What are your biggest takeaways from today's session?'

Although their response is helpful for the coachee, I also find it invaluable for me as the coach. I have learned many things by asking this question, not least that I cannot always accurately judge my own coaching effectiveness. Many times, I have asked this question and been pleasantly surprised, even delighted, by the answers I have received. On occasion I have worried that a session has not have been impactful enough, only to hear my coachee describe how helpful it has been to talk things through and get their thoughts straight in their head. Conversely, there have also been a few times when I have felt a session has gone well, only for the coachee to disclose that we haven't really covered what they wanted to discuss.

This can sometimes be frustrating or perplexing to hear, but it is valuable feedback nonetheless, and has prompted some useful self-reflection for me.

Although their replies offer immediate feedback, whether that be reassurance or points for development, it also has a far greater value: by reflecting on the replies received over the years, I have learned what people really value about coaching, and about me as a coach. It has given me a sense of what my coachees most need from me and where my personal strengths lie. Their answers have made me a better coach.

As you become more confident and experienced as a coach, you will find your own way of asking this final summation question. Alternatives to 'What are your biggest takeaways from today's session?' include:

- What will you remember from today's session?

- What has been the most valuable element of our time together today?

- What have you learned today and what has been most helpful?

- What will you do differently going forward because of our coaching?

- Which aspects of our work today did you most enjoy?

- What are you most looking forward to putting into practice?

However you choose to phrase this fundamental question that indicates the completion of our MAGIC questioning arc, remember its function is also in bringing each session to a positive, constructive close. As one session closes, we then link forward to the timing and theme for our next, where the MAGIC questioning arc will begin again, and an opportunity for us to see how the magic has happened in the silence between our sessions.

A final tip learned through my own experience: if you schedule several sessions in a day, I recommend that you always leave yourself sufficient breathing space between. This is important on a practical level, to enable you to write up your notes from the previous session and prepare for the next, but also on a personal level, to enable you to recharge and renew your own energy. It is helpful for you to create a symbolic gap between sessions. You might step outside and take a few deep breaths, go for a short walk, have a snack or listen to some music. Whatever you choose to do to create the gap, I really recommend that you build this into your timetable, for the benefit of you and your coachees. This space, too, is a magical silence.

18
One Bonus Question
Can you tell me more...?

We have now covered the fifteen questions that form the questioning arc of our MAGIC Methodology, but before we finish this section, here is one bonus question, 'Can you tell me more...?' This may be the best coaching question of all time. It is as beautiful as it is simple.

If you sense your coachee has more share with you, but you don't want just to repeat your previous question, or you feel that they may respond better if prompted slightly differently, now is the moment to simply ask, 'Can you tell me more...?'

If they come up with an idea which you think is unrealistic or unachievable, all you need to ask is, 'Can you tell me more...?' As they talk, you can together explore if there are any grounds for your concerns.

If you find yourself making assumptions and are concerned that your own inherent and unavoidable biases and assumptions may be influencing the questioning, again, you can just ask, 'Can you tell me more...?' It is a beautifully neutral question which gives the coachee freedom to respond in their own way, while you take a moment to check your response.

Quite simply, you can ask a version of this question at any stage. It is a close relation of the AWE question, 'And what else...?' that we mentioned in the Ideas section. If you feel stuck and don't know what to say next, just ask, 'Can you tell me more...?' or 'Go on...?', or even just 'And...?' and follow this with a pause. Sometimes it is most powerful just to say nothing at all. Nod, smile, pause and wait as the magic happens in the silence.

PART THREE
MAKING THE MAGIC HAPPEN

19
What Happens Next?

W e've now covered the entire MAGIC Methodology in Part Two of this book, working within
a framework of fifteen reflective questions (and an
extra bonus question). We've examined the significance and potential of each question and, along the
way, we've introduced a wide range of coaching tools
and techniques that will add variety and depth to our
coaching. Now it is time to complete our journey by
considering what happens next... how do we *really*
make the magic happen?

As you practise the MAGIC Methodology more and
begin to make it your own, your maturing coaching
skills will support and assist your coachees to reach
their goals more successfully and more frequently,
and you will grow as a coach. You will become more

confident, capable and effective at facilitating magic results for yourself and your coachees.

In this final section of the book, we are going to look at three practical aspects of how to make this magic happen, with some insights, thoughts and suggestions to help you consider how to move forward using the knowledge we have shared:

- How to use MAGIC to build a coaching programme

- How to use MAGIC to be your own coach

- How to continue your personal development as a MAGIC coach

20

How To Use MAGIC To Build A Coaching Programme

One of the beauties of the MAGIC Methodology, as I mentioned at the beginning of this book, is how incredibly flexible it is in its application. It can be used to give an effective framework to a single coaching session or, equally, to structure a complete coaching programme that runs over several sessions. It is always applicable and scalable, no matter the amount of time available, and its use will enable you to make the most of whatever time you have.

Now that you are familiar with the methodology, let's look at how we can use it to design our sessions to create a cohesive programme, regardless of the time available.

Suggested plan for an hour-long session

In an ongoing coaching programme, the approximate flow of an hour's session could look like this:

Open	10 minutes	Welcome, check-in, rapport building.
		How are they? What's new?
Review	10 minutes	What can they remember from last time?
		What were their actions?
		What progress have they made?
Theme	30 minutes	Agree the theme for today, depending on where you are in the MAGIC process.
		Ask lots of questions, listen well, agree some outputs.
Close	10 minutes	Recap key points from the session.
		What are their main takeaways?
		What is the first thing they will do when they leave today?
		What did they find the most useful part of today's session?
		When will you meet again?

Suggested plan for a four-session programme

Here is a suggestion for a typical coaching programme that can be adapted to any topic and goal; on this occasion, we are spacing the MAGIC framework over four coaching sessions, preceded by an initial 'discovery' meeting, with a specific theme each time, as you move systematically through the process.

Pre-coaching session

The theme of this first session is **discovery**.

Before a coaching relationship formally begins, I recommend that you arrange an introductory meeting where you can get to know each other. There needs to be a certain connection between you for the relationship to work, so this is sometimes referred to as a 'chemistry' session.

The purpose of this session is three-fold:

1. **Rapport building:** You both need to establish if you are good match, and you will need to be sure that you have the skills and expertise to help them with your coaching. For the coachee, it is common practice to speak to several potential coaches before they choose who to work with. If they elect to work with you as their coach, this meeting helps you to plan your programme, understand their aspirations and goals, and consider which approach could create the best coaching environment for them.

2. **Contracting:** This meeting is to discuss how you could work together. If you are an independent coach, you will need to agree the terms and conditions of a formal contract. What is the scope of the coaching, what are the financial arrangements, and what happens if they need to cancel, rearrange or terminate the coaching? If you are working within an organisational context, you can use this meeting to establish an informal 'ways-of-working' contract between the two of you, perhaps discussing issues such as openness and confidentiality.

3. **Sales:** For an independent coach, this is ultimately a sales meeting. Will you win this piece of business? Can you clearly and effectively articulate the benefits of your coaching over that of others? You won't be the right coach for everyone and it is important to recognise this, so be clear about what you offer and for whom, and you will find that you attract these ideal clients. Recommendations will come from people who understand and like what you do, and your website, marketing, networking and history of success record will connect with a certain group who are looking for what you offer.

During a discovery session, you can go through the MAGIC Methodology at a high overview level, using our questioning arc as a guide, to gain a good understanding of the prospective coachee's current situation, what they would like to achieve, what ideas they already have about how to move forward, and how committed they are to the coaching process. The aim of this session is essentially to demonstrate the value of coaching, to hint at potential new insights and enhanced self-awareness and to generate some excitement about the journey upon which they are now embarking.

Session 1

The theme of this session is **Mirror.**

This is your first coaching session of the programme proper, so you now begin to work through the first stage of our MAGIC Methodology. This will enable you to explore your coachee's current situation in detail, what is going well and not so well, where they are satisfied and where they are not, and what has motivated them to seek out coaching now. Tools such as the Magic Wheel exercise can be invaluable within this crucial opening session to establish a baseline and starting point.

Session 2

This second coaching session within the programme explores their **Aspirations** and **Goals**. The aim is to clarify some SMART goals that will be used to measure the success of the coaching, and the tools and techniques we covered in the corresponding sections will guide you here.

As we have learned, it is crucial that we don't assume that a coachee already knows what they want when we start coaching. Many coachees assert clearly defined goals, but it is always, *always*, worth delving deeper to explore why they have chosen their goal and how the reality will look and feel once it has been achieved. Many coachees will refine, reshape and sometimes totally change their goal during this process; if they don't, great – your questions will have confirmed that this is indeed the right goal, and re-affirmed why.

Session 3

This is the **Ideas** and **Commitments** session. It should be used to explore potential options and then create a workable and well-defined plan to help the coachee plot the journey across the bridge, from their current situation to the destination of their aspirations and goals, again using a number of the tools and techniques we have explored.

Session 4

This is the **review and next steps** session, which can be used to recap key learning, review progress, explore barriers and obstacles and plan out next steps. It can work well to revisit tools used in the opening session to explore the progress they have made. If their scores have already improved, it can be hugely motivating to see this laid out as clear evidence of their achievements.

If their scores have not yet improved, do not let them become disheartened: the MAGIC Methodology is a cyclical and endlessly repeatable framework; some improvements will take time to come to fruition, but the coaching has begun this process.

When you are discussing what has been most useful, a great idea at this stage is to agree on a few final assignments to keep the momentum going. Here are some possible tasks:

- Review their notes to appreciate their progress and then explore what has been the most useful elements of the coaching.

- Plan something to celebrate their achievements or launch the next stage of their journey, something which feels special, maybe a nice meal, a personal treat or a fun event.

Optional follow-up session: It is also a good idea to discuss a follow-up discussion, perhaps after several months, to review further progress and maintain the momentum from the coaching.

Key principles for ongoing coaching

However you choose to plan your coaching programme, here are three key principles that I'd recommend that you follow, for any ongoing programme.

Begin every session by 'checking in'

Always start by checking in with your coachee to see how they are and what's new. Many times, I have had my beautiful plan completely blown out of the water because a coachee has arrived with a much more pressing problem upon which they want to focus. We need to go with this and follow their agenda, because if we don't, they won't be concentrating anyway. This is where your emotional intelligence and ability to be flexible will stand you in good stead.

If you have already agreed one agenda, and they are now presenting a different challenge to discuss, I suggest that you lay this out and ask them what they would like to do now. Provide a simple overview of the situation as you understand it (a chance to confirm that you have understood correctly) and give them a choice so that the programme remains coachee-led: 'We had agreed to discuss *xyz* today, but it seems like *abc* is on your mind. How would you like to use the time we have together today?'

Always review the previous session

It is excellent practice to start by asking the coachee to reflect on their key takeaways from last time and their progress since. Remind your coachee what you discussed, the actions they committed themselves to and ask about the progress they have made since you last met; even better, ask them to do this recap of your last session themselves. This has several benefits. It focuses them back onto the coaching, reminds you both of where you got to, and importantly, when they realise that you will do this every time, it provides extra motivation for them to carry out their commitments as planned as they know they will be held to account.

Plan a different theme for each session

Planning a different theme helps each session develop its own personality or character, so that they don't all blend into one. I also try to incorporate at least one exercise into each session, to add variety and colour. This is particularly useful with coachees who work with high energy and move at a fast pace.

I have demonstrated the beautiful flexibility of the MAGIC Methodology, equally applicable as a tool to guide you through a single hour or an ongoing multi-session coaching programme. As I have become more experienced as a coach, I have grown ever stronger in my belief in the power of following a structure. I have realised that having a clear framework to follow does not impede flexibility; I find that it gives you the freedom to flow.

21

How To Use MAGIC To Be Your Own Coach

We have so far discussed how to use the MAGIC Methodology when coaching others, but it can also work surprisingly well as a tool to coach ourselves, working through the questions in the same systematic way and engaging with a range of the exercises we have discussed.

If you choose to try this, it is important to carve out sufficient time to do this properly. If you were going to commission a coach, you would set aside dedicated time for it, so if you are going to be your own coach, you need to do the same. Perhaps you can diarise a dedicated weekly or fortnightly slot to ensure the time is set aside? Remember to think about the requirements of place as well as time: find a space where you can focus and contemplate, somewhere quiet and free from distractions.

It can also help to consider your personal style and think about how you like to learn and process information. Are you someone who, like me, loves words? Do you enjoy writing and expressing yourself on paper? Everyone loves new stationery, so this could be a great time to indulge in the perfect notebook to record your thoughts as you work through the questions. Perhaps you are a visual thinker? Would it help to create pictures, graphics and diagrams? Do you prefer to work with technology? Is there an app or piece of software which you could use to schematise your thoughts? Could a simple spreadsheet fit the bill?

Are you an outdoors person? My husband thinks best when he is on his feet. I can always tell that he is deep in thought when I look out the window and see him ambling round the garden. If he needs to have a challenging conversation, he will always get up and walk around, so if he has his phone in his hand as he paces our garden, I know that this is a discussion that requires proper concentration. If you too can relate to this, it could work well for you to be move around while you think. Could you go for a walk, run, bike ride or drive while you ponder one of our questions? Some coaches have started to offer walking coaching sessions and this certainly appeals to me.

Are you externally or internally motivated? If you know you have fantastic self-control and self-motivation, then simply setting yourself a goal or a deadline might be enough to keep you laser-focused on achieving it. If you need more external motivation, you could share your goals and deadlines with a friend, colleague or family member who can act as your buddy, checking in to support you and holding you to account. The important thing is simply to choose a way of self-coaching which works for you, reflects your own learning style and plays to your strengths.

Once you have decided how to proceed, you can then start to coach yourself just as you would coach someone else. My advice is to work systematically through the coaching questions in the MAGIC framework, asking yourself one question at a time and taking your time before moving on. You need to allow time to explore and consider your answer, but also allow space between these active reflection sessions when your mind can wander freely and unconstrained – this is your 'silence' and we know that this is when the magic happens. You might take one question per session, or you may work through the whole framework in one sitting. There is no right or wrong here. Choose what works for you, and don't rush. Don't forget to record all your answers and celebrate all your successes. You may just surprise yourself.

22

How To Continue Your Personal Development As A MAGIC Coach

As we approach the end of the book, I have some final suggestions to share that will further enhance your growth as a coach. You will be familiar by now with the core elements of effective coaching, so this is about engaging in a process of continuous personal development to enhance the knowledge, skills and behaviours which will be vital to your success.

Final thoughts on your personal development

I'm going to conclude our consideration of how to continue your personal development as a MAGIC coach by introducing three further actions you could take to help you manage and measure your progress:

- Enhance your questioning and listening skills.

- Keep good records.

- Engage in reflective practice.

Enhance your questioning and listening skills

As you become more comfortable with using the MAGIC framework, you will begin to make it your own, perhaps adding in your own questions or slight variations. I would therefore suggest that developing your questioning and listening skills is one of the most effective ways to enhance your personal growth as a coach.

To improve the quality of the questions we ask, it really helps to think about your purpose, always considering why you are asking each question and where you are hoping it will take you. Every question has the potential to take you somewhere new: some will take you further down the path you are already travelling while others will take you in a totally different, and maybe better, direction; a few may take you down a dead end, and others might take you back down a path you have previously travelled. Consider the potential impact of the answers before making a conscious decision that this is the right question to ask and the right time.

When we ask questions, it is clearly crucial that we actively and openly listen to the answers. This may sound obvious but when we feel under pressure as a coach, listening is often the first behaviour to disappear out of the window as we worry about time and the quality of our coaching. Working to improve your questioning and listening skills will be an essential component of your personal development as a coach.

Keep good records

Write it all down! A key aspect of demonstrating professionalism and enhancing your effectiveness is keeping systematic and comprehensive records of your coaching activity and storing them safely. This will provide a record for you to refer to as the coaching progresses, improving continuity between sessions and enabling you to evaluate progress. In the workplace, good records capture evidence to be used in performance management and demonstrate achievement against objectives.

Along with your coaching contract that clarifies the term and conditions you have agreed with each coachee, your records should contain the time, date and place of each coaching session, plus a succinct summary of the discussion, outcomes and agreed actions. It is also critical that you familiarise yourself with the most up to date data protection legislation, as requirements can change over time.

Engage in reflective practice

Reflective practice is the habit of mindfully thinking back over the previous coaching sessions, in a structured and consistent way, using the feedback from your coachees plus your own notes and observations. I thoroughly recommend that you keep a coaching journal to record your reflections, which you can read periodically to enable you to learn over time and see your development.

During your reflective practice, you can analyse your strengths and development areas, considering what went well and what you think you could have done differently; although this will primarily be from your professional experiences, it is also worth thinking more broadly to consider what you have learned about yourself and why. This engages you in a process of continuous learning and growth, to ensure that you become the strongest coach that you can be, and that your coachees benefit from the best coaching that you can give.

We can engage in solo reflective practice and that is beneficial, but I would also recommend that anyone who coaches regularly finds themselves a supervisor to work with, to create a safe and confidential space to explore your coaching with a skilled and experienced expert. They can hold the mirror up for you, as you have done for your coachees, assisting you in your self-reflection and providing an objective and unbiased view. This enables you to review practice, seek support and guidance if you need it, explore any unconscious behaviours that may impact your coaching, and reveal skills gaps that can inform your professional growth. This, in turn, helps maintain and raise standards across the whole coaching profession.

Conclusion

With these final thoughts, we now move to the end of our journey. We have covered a lot of ground, and I hope you have enjoyed reading this as much as I have enjoyed writing it.

We began with an introduction to coaching, exploring definitions of coaching, the role of a coach and some of its wonderful and wide-ranging benefits.

We have walked systematically through our MAGIC Methodology with its powerful questioning arc, and we have delved deep into the rationale behind each of the carefully chosen questions. I have shared a range of tools and techniques to help add variety, colour and depth to your sessions and to enhance the value, impact and success of your coaching. We have seen how the MAGIC Methodology can be usefully applied to any coaching, regardless of length, and demonstrated how it can help add structure and focus through the process.

We have explored a way to use MAGIC to be your own coach, applying the methodology to help you achieve your own aspirations and goals, and finally we have looked at some next steps for you as a coach, to help you develop your skills, and enhance your success. The aim of this book has been to inspire you with a glimpse into the incredible power of coaching, to build your skills and your confidence, and to encourage you to explore the rich potential of the coaching principles in both your personal and your professional life.

I am convinced that coaching has a vital role to play in the modern world, at work and in our personal lives. If we can help our coachees to better understand themselves and their personal situations – to explore their aspirations, clarify their goals, create plans and ultimately to achieve success, whatever that means for them – then that is an amazing contribution that we can make as coaches.

However you choose to use the MAGIC Methodology, and whether to coach yourself or others, I wish you every success moving forward. I'm confident the techniques will work brilliantly for you, and I would love to hear how you get on.

Bibliography

Adams, D and M Carwardine, *Last Chance To See* (Ballantine Books, 1990)

'Art', *Collins English Dictionary* (no date), www. collinsdictionary.com/dictionary/english/art, accessed May 2022

Author unknown, *Tao Te Ching*, publication date unknown, proverb is from Chapter 64; 'Tao Te Ching', *Wikipedia* (last edited May 2022), https:// en.wikipedia.org/wiki/Tao_Te_Ching, accessed May 2022

Author unknown, 'Is "The beginning is half of every action" truly a Greek proverb?', Latin Language Stack Exchange (December 2019),

https://latin.stackexchange.com/questions/12900/
is-the-beginning-is-half-of-every-action-truly-a-
greek-proverb, accessed May 2022

Berger, W, *A More Beautiful Question: The power of
inquiry to spark breakthrough ideas* (Bloomsbury USA,
2014)

Carnegie, D, *How To Win Friends And Influence People*
(Vermilion, 2012)

Conan Doyle, A, 'A Scandal in Bohemia', *The Strand
Magazine*, 2 (July 1891), 61–75; www.arthur-conan-
doyle.com/index.php?title=A_Scandal_in_Bohemia,
accessed May 2022

Covey, S, *The 7 Habits of Highly Effective People:
Powerful lessons in personal change* (Simon & Schuster
UK Ltd, 1989)

De Bono, E, *Six Thinking Hats: An essential approach
to business management* (Little, Brown and Company,
1985)

Doran, G, 'There's a S.M.A.R.T. way to write
management's goals and objectives', *Management
Review*, 70/11 (November 1981), 35–36, https://
community.mis.temple.edu/mis0855002fall2015/
files/2015/10/S.M.A.R.T-Way-Management-Review.
pdf, accessed May 2022

Gallup, Learn about the Science of CliftonStrengths (Gallup, 2022), https://gallup.com/cliftonstrengths/en/253790/science-of-cliftonstrengths.aspx, accessed May 2022

Gallwey, WT, *The Inner Game Of Tennis* (Random House Inc, 1974)

Gladwell, M, *The Outliers: The story of success* (Penguin Books, 2009)

Goleman, D, *Emotional Intelligence: Why it can matter more than IQ* (Bloomsbury Publishing, 1995)

Henwood, S, *The Top 5 Tips for Understanding your Values* (The Association for Coaching, no date), https://cdn.ymaws.com/associationforcoaching. site-ym.com/resource/resmgr/Articles_&_ Handy_Guides/Coaches/Handy_Guides/ Top_5_tips_for_understanding.pdf, accessed May 2022

Jeffers, S, *Feel The Fear And Do It Anyway: Dynamic techniques for turning fear, indecision, and anger into power, action, and love* (Fawcett Columbine Books, 1988)

Kemp, N, 'Ikigai misunderstood and the origin of the Ikigai Venn diagram', Ikigai Tribe (23 July 2019), https://ikigaitribe.com/ikigai/ikigai-misunderstood, accessed May 2022

Kemp, N, 'Mieko Kamiya – the Mother of Ikigai psychology', Ikigai Tribe (23 March 2020), https://ikigaitribe.com/ikigai/mieko-kamiya, accessed May 2022

Kline, N, *Time to Think: Listening to ignite the human mind* (Cassell, 2002)

Landsberg, M, *The Tao of Coaching: Boost your effectiveness at work by inspiring and developing those around you* (IPS Profile Books, 1996)

Monkton, E, *Life: The interesting thoughts of Edward Monkton* (HarperCollins Publishers, 2005)

Morgan, K, *Overcoming Imposter Syndrome in Your Coaching Business* (International Coaching Federation, 2018), https://coachingfederation.org/blog/overcoming-impostor-syndrome-in-your-coaching-business, accessed May 2022

Mitsuhashi, Y, 'Ikigai: A Japanese concept to improve work and life', *BBC Worklife* (8 August 2017), www.bbc.com/worklife/article/20170807-ikigai-a-japanese-concept-to-improve-work-and-life, accessed May 2022

Murphy, S, 'Future Protocol, a.k.a. Back to the Future', School Reform Initiative: A community of learners (August 2002; revised June 2008), http://school

reforminitiative.org/doc/future.pdf, accessed May 2022

Newton, I, and R Hooke, 'Isaac Newton letter to Robert Hooke, 1675', Historical Society of Pennsylvania (6 February 1675), https://discover. hsp.org/Record/dc-9792, accessed May 2022

O'Toole, G, 'If you always do what you've always done, you always get what you've always gotten', *Quote Investigator* (25 April 2016), https://quoteinvestigator. com/2016/04/25/get, accessed May 2022

O'Toole, G, 'Insanity is doing the same thing over and over again and expecting different results', *Quote Investigator* (23 March 2017), https:// quoteinvestigator.com/2017/03/23/same, accessed May 2022

Ries, E, *The Lean Startup: How today's entrepreneurs use continuous innovation to create radically successful businesses* (Portfolio Penguin, 2011)

Robbins, A, *Unlimited Power: The new science of personal achievement* (Simon & Schuster UK, 2001)

Rubinstein, P, 'The hidden upside of imposter syndrome', *BBC Worklife* (17 March 2021), www.bbc. com/worklife/article/20210315-the-hidden-upside-of-imposter-syndrome, accessed May 2022

Ryan, A, *This Year I Will… How to finally change a habit, keep a resolution, or make a dream come true* (Broadway Books, 2006)

Sinek, S, *Start With Why: The inspiring million-copy bestseller that will help you find your purpose* (Penguin Books Ltd, 2011)

Smith, E, *Luck: A Fresh Look at Fortune* (Bloomsbury Paperbacks, 2013)

Stanier, MB, *The Coaching Habit: Say Less, Ask More & Change the Way You Lead Forever* (Page Two, 2016)

'Unconscious bias', *Collins English Dictionary* (no date), www.collinsdictionary.com/dictionary/english/unconscious_bias, accessed May 2022 Thesaurus.com, *The 100 Most Common Words in English* (Thesaurus.com, 2020), https://thesaurus.com/e/writing/common-words/, accessed May 2022

Whitmore, J, *GROWing Human Potential And Purpose: The principles and practice of coaching and leadership* (Nicholas Brealey Publishing, 1992)

Acknowledgements

My thanks go to my three wonderful children, Emily, Sam and Ben, who have been the catalyst for my whole journey. Their arrival was my motivation for leaving corporate life and branching out solo, in a bid to balance fulfilling and meaningful work with being present for my family, and my company. ESB Training & Coaching Consultancy, is named after them. That you can read this book now is down to Emily, who first emboldened me to send my manuscript out to gather feedback – without her, it might still be a Word document on my laptop. Watching their own personal journeys as they grow and spread their wings is a constant delight.

My deepest thanks to my lovely husband Greg, who is endlessly supportive of the work that I do – and indeed everything that I do. Thanks are due also to my lovely stepdaughters, Emily, Molly and Katie (yes it can be confusing to have two daughters called Emily!) who joined our family many years ago, bringing so much joy and general loveliness with them.

Huge thanks to Jan Doyle, who has been my closest colleague for fifteen years and one of the earliest readers of this book. I have learned so much from Jan and her wealth of wisdom and experience: long may our collaboration continue.

Thank you so much to Charlotte Hurst and Jo Richards. I found it terrifying to send my early drafts out to you to read, but your positive responses gave me the encouragement to carry on and your comments were incredibly helpful. I also want to give enormous thanks to Pete Masters for investing a significant amount of time in going through the whole manuscript with a fantastic attention to detail and providing such insightful and constructive input, and for writing the Foreword. It is a much better book because of all of you.

My thanks also to my wonderful 'Coaches & Coffee' group, who have tested my coaching framework for me, shared heaps of invaluable advice and experience, and helped to create a warm community of local coaches, providing encouragement in a profession that can sometimes feel isolating, working alone but providing support to others. This has helped clarify one of my more recent discoveries, which has been the beauty of group coaching. My next book is devoted to helping you unleash its special power: *The MAGIC Happens Round the Table* is coming soon.

For line managers, we recognise that coaching to achieve organisational goals requires a special focus for your skills, and there is a book in the pipeline for you too: *Magic for Managers*.

At ESB Training, we offer a range of training and coaching services and would be delighted to work with you to help you achieve individual or organisational success. Visit my website to find out more at www.esb-training.co.uk

The Author

Rosie Nice studied History at the University of Cambridge before joining British Airways on their Graduate Development Programme, where she spent several happy years.

During her time at British Airways, in every role she held, she found herself gravitating towards projects which focused on people development. She found herself amazed and fascinated by the transformations she observed in people who had been coached, trained and invested in, and therefore decided to devote her career to helping untap people's hidden potential and supporting individuals, teams and organisations in achieving excellence.

In 1997 she founded ESB Training & Coaching Consultancy and she has now been an independent consultant for over twenty years. Her focus is on helping coaches and managers become confident, competent, qualified and successful. This book has enabled her to share many of the lessons she has learned along the way.

⊕ www.esb-training.co.uk

▥ www.linkedin.com/in/rosienice

▨ @esbtraining

Printed in Great Britain
by Amazon

86526796R00150